i

This Season of Hope

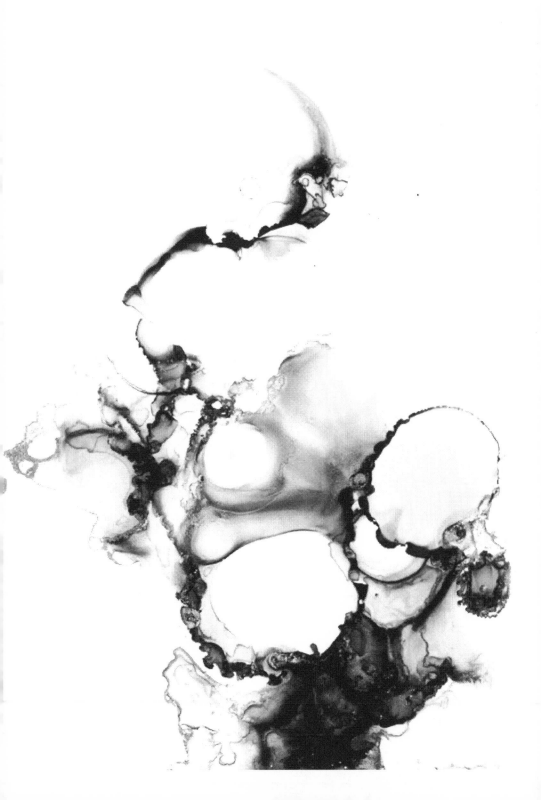

This Season of Hope

5-Minute Messages to Recapture the Life You Were Designed to Live

Paula Ann Lambert

Cover Art courtesy of Kendra Neal

Hand Lettering by Monica Ebersole

Photography by The Beautiful Mess

Hair by Amy Hayes

Table of Contents

Acknowledgements   viii

About This Devotional   ix

A Note from the Author   xi

Endorsements   xii

Dedication   xv

1- Justice, Mercy, and Grace   1

2- Change Your Filter   5

3- If God is Sovereign, Why Pray?   8

4- Why Didn't God Make Us Robots?   11

5- Draw A Circle   14

6- Reconcile My Life   17

7- The 80/20 Rule   20

8- Less Than or Equal To?   23

9- What Will They Say When I'm Gone?   27

10- Sharpen Your Ax   31

11- Mother's Day   34

12- Roller Coaster Days   37

13- Hidden Figures   41

14- Only God Makes Things Grow   44

15- Your Own Skin   47

16- This Season of Hope   50

17- Road Through the Desert   53

18- State of Forgiveness   56

19- Responsibility   59

20- Skeleton in My Closet   62

21- Bang Your Head   67

22- The Sheep and The Goats   70

23- Run Out of The Grave   73

24- Travel Light   77

25- Love Divine   80

26- Double Agent   83

27- Border Patrol   86

28- End Game   89

29- Grateful, Thankful, Blessed   93

30- Comfort and Joy   97

31- Losing My Religion   100

Index of Topics   104

References   105

About the Author   107

Thank You   108

Acknowledgements

Editor - Holly Murray
Hand Lettering, Interior Art, and Cover Design - Meagan Lambert

Contributors:

Anonymous by permission, "Run Out of the Grave"
Christan Barnett, 28Bold, "Grateful, Thankful, Blessed"
Ginny Murray, "Skeleton in My Closet"
Cathy Pizarro, "What Will They Say When I'm Gone?"

About This Devotional

Between these pages I hope you can find something that inspires and encourages you! You can use this devotional in different ways; a personal study that goes day by day (or in any order) or an informal bible study that you can share with your friends and have conversations about each topic. However you choose to use it, my prayer is that these words would be beneficial to you! This is a personal devotion designed to set the main idea backed up with scripture and followed up with prayer and action to help you make whatever change is necessary.

These devotions are crafted to be thought-provoking and to push you to action. If we don't know what the problem is, we cannot work on it. Hopefully, after delving into a few of these short topics you will be able to self-reflect and systematically get to the heart of issues that possibly hold you back from whatever it is that God has planned for you. Issues that may have plagued you for years may be addressed.

Make sure you jot down the date on each devotional so that you can come back later and rejoice for answered prayer. Ultimately, I pray you would be equipped with the Word to surmount any current or future issues you face and find hope and strength from the Lord in this season. The Word says, "but those who hope in the Lord will renew their strength" (Isaiah 40:31 NIV).

Most of these concepts came from real-life first-hand experiences of my own and there are a few stories from friends who gave their permission to share them with you. In fact, if you are reading this, I consider us friends!

You must know above all that you are important, and you matter to God. I'm thrilled that you are on this journey with me, and I pray that every hand this book touches is blessed with unexplainable blessings!

This Season of Hope

A Note from the Author

I'm excited to share with you some places in my life where God has directed me and taught me some spiritual truths. I am in no way perfect and make mistakes daily. My prayer is that you would find something within these pages that is relatable, that would inspire and encourage you on your journey.

I've said many times that we can study the Bible and be learned biblical scholars, but unless and until we apply the principles within the Word, we will unfortunately remain fools.

I firmly believe you will find more joy, hope, and freedom living with Jesus in your life than you would otherwise.

If you have not accepted Jesus as your personal Savior or are new to the Christian faith, I encourage you to stop and pray this simple prayer of salvation right now wherever you are. No other decision in your life will be as important as this one.

Dear Jesus,

I give You my life today and I give You ultimate control. I ask for forgiveness for every sin I ever committed, and I believe You will walk with me and give me strength to make good decisions from this point forward. I accept You as my personal Savior and I will follow You.

Amen.

Congratulations on making the best decision of your life! Now, tell a friend and encourage each other as you go.

Endorsements

"In our fast-paced, stress-filled world, it's easy to rush through an entire day without pausing to connect with God and recharge our souls. *This Season of Hope* is more than just a devotional; it's a daily refuge for your soul and a daily opportunity to connect with your Creator. Paula has crafted a beautiful biblical resource that will be a powerful source of encouragement, inspiration, and hope for all who read it. These daily devotionals might become the most important five minutes of your entire day."
-Dave Willis
Pastor and Bestselling Author, Marriage Today
Keller, Texas

"I've known Paula and her husband Jerry through many seasons – both of life and ministry. I'm so glad she took the time to write about her experiences. She offers a unique and fresh perspective for women through daily devotionals that will not only encourage you, but give you that nudge you need to push through whatever season you find yourself in."
-Marty Baker
Lead Pastor, Stevens Creek Church
Augusta, Georgia

"In *This Season of Hope,* Paula is incredibly transparent about what she has learned in real life situations, which makes an instant connection with the reader. She aptly ties in the truths of God's Word and asks thought-provoking questions that make for an attractive go-to daily devotional. She keeps it real!"
-Leah Sustar
Lead Pastor's Wife, High Praises Church
Anderson, South Carolina

"Inspirational, informative, and challenging! These are the first few words that come to mind when I read from *This Season of Hope*. I'm always on the lookout for a good daily devotional. The opportunity to be inspired, informed, and challenged by a short chapter from a well-written book is a great way to start the day. Paula Lambert gives us encouragement, nourishment, and motivation to grow in this compilation of Scripture, powerful quotes, and interesting short stories. I heartily recommend this as an addition to your daily intake of information."

-Rich Bowen
Senior Pastor, New Hope Worship Center
Grovetown, Georgia

"Honest and persistent, Paula Lambert is a woman unafraid to be in the trenches of life with those she loves. Because she has lived a faith that seeks to demonstrate the goodness of God while acknowledging the journey can get downright crazy some days, you will find her reflections to be not only transparent and genuine but also practical. *This Season of Hope* presents the struggles we have all faced, either personally or with those we love. Enjoy the journey, reader, and may you see the unmistakable hand of God moving in your life as you reach toward this invitation to believe that with God the impossible becomes our reality.

-Regina Franklin
Author of *Who Calls Me Beautiful?*
Thomson, Georgia

"If you have ever asked the questions, "Does anyone understand? Does anyone care? Who on earth will come alongside me and help me?", then Paula's biblical-focused devotional is lovingly written especially for you! Grab your Bible, a copy of *This Season of Hope*, and good ol' cup of hot tea, and get ready to transform your life as you take practical action daily, while rightly dividing God's Word of Truth."

-Tina LaRea
Author of *In Her Shoes, Unleash the Sparkle of Survival*
Scottsdale, Arizona

"Paula offers encouragement that testifies to the love and faithfulness of God. *This Season of Hope* gives timeless wisdom and inspiration that will strengthen your faith. As Paula communicates from her heart to the reader, you immediately feel like you are having a conversation. You will relate to the honesty in each day's devotion and then be challenged to apply important biblical truth.

Thank you, Paula, for showing us how to "put action behind our dreams and goals to make them happen." Your dream to write this devotional book is a gift to the reader that we will want to share with family and friends."

-Gina Anderson
Director, East Texas Center for Nonprofits and
Lead Pastor's Wife, Rose Heights Church
Tyler, Texas

Dedication

I dedicate this book to my family and friends. You've been patient for the better part of a year and have been the fuel that helped this little devotional-that-could pull out of the station!

To my brilliant husband, Jerry, for whom my heart still beats. Without you I could not have walked these many places from which my stories came. I love you.

To my daughters, Christan and Meagan - the two women in my life whom I have learned the most from. I couldn't have dreamed the impact you both have already made on the world.

To my son in law, David. You are still number one. Thank you for being a good man and devoted father to Harrison, Collins, and Baylor.

To my parents, Joe and Loretta Winn. You are my oldest friends. You've seen me at my worst and you've seen me at my best. Thank you for giving me life, teaching me, and modeling so many of the principles that are forever imprinted in my heart. Thank you for always being in my corner.

To my sisters, Sherrie and Elle. No matter the distance, my heart crosses the miles between us every day. You are both an inspiration now and always.

To the many friends who are involved in these stories and more to come, I love you truly, madly, deeply. Thank you for just letting me be me. I enjoy you!

1- Justice, Mercy, and Grace

"... And what does the Lord require of you?
To act justly and to love mercy
and to walk humbly with your God."
Micah 6:8 NIV

My closest friends know I haven't always been a rule follower. It's true I guess to some degree. I often push the limits of whatever I'm confronted with. As you might imagine, this approach has not always worked out very well.

While on a weekender at the beach with some great friends, we were looking for a place to have dinner. As the driver, I was attempting to follow the GPS on my phone and when the voice on the GPS said, "you have arrived," we saw nothing. In the location where we expected to see the restaurant, there was literally no building at all.

We all found this to be quite humorous. It was biker's week at the beach and we were in the middle of heavy traffic. Still processing the missing restaurant and trying to figure out where to go next, I saw the traffic light turn yellow. I continued driving through the intersection as the light was also turning a beautiful hue of red. My friend in the passenger's seat said, "those are blue lights behind you. Pull over and hand me your phone."

Reality set in. I felt the serious responsibility of the moment and it was very sobering. Referring to the officer who was approaching the vehicle, I said, "I hope he's in a good mood." After the officer approached the vehicle and asked for the license and registration he said, "Well, I'm in a good mood today." Yay! He was so nice and decided to only give me a warning!

After I had a little time to think about what had just happened, I went to the spiritual place in my mind and said, "I didn't get what I deserved. Thank you, Lord, for mercy." I was truly thankful. I honestly should have gotten a ticket. I clearly broke the law and I was keenly aware of the possible consequences. An expensive ticket would have just killed the good mood for the rest of the weekend.

Instead of a ticket, though, I received a lesson in justice, mercy, and grace. Justice would mean that I would have gotten a pricy ticket for the standard amount for running a red light. That would be what I deserved. Instead, I didn't get what I deserved. I received mercy in the form of forgiveness and no ticket. Grace, getting what I don't deserve, was what I received from my friends. Instead of being angry, they were able to get a good laugh about that experience. Actually, they will probably never let me live that down!

A short two weeks later I was at a different beach with a different group of friends. I had parked the car near the beach access. Returning to the car after an absolutely perfect day, I discovered a ticket on my windshield! In the margin handwritten were the words "$100 fee upon next violation."

My first thought was, "What?!" I hadn't even realized it, but I was in a reserved parking section. On the dashboard, I had placed the pass that allowed admittance to the condo, and I thought that it covered all the parking areas. Apparently, it did not. And while ignorance is no excuse for breaking the law, mercy had been extended to me once again.

Everybody wants justice when it's for someone else. When it comes to us, we prefer mercy and grace. I deserved justice. Fortunately for us, God is also a God of mercy and grace. That knowledge gives us hope in the most uncomfortable situations. We may warrant the cuffs of justice and long for the relief of mercy, but God generously gifts grace to the undeserving. What a compassionate God we have!

"Therefore the Lord longs to be gracious to you,
And therefore He waits on high to have compassion on you.
For the Lord is a God of justice;
How blessed are all those who long for Him."
Isaiah 30:18 NASB

Paula Lambert

*"But because of His great love for us,
God, who is rich in mercy, made us alive with Christ even
when we were dead in transgressions –
it is by grace you have been saved."
Ephesians 2:4-5 NIV*

Act Justly. love Mercy. walk humbly before God.

Name a situation where God gave you mercy or grace. Name a situation where you can exercise grace for someone else.

Notes:

_____

_____

_____

_____

_____

2- Change Your Filter

"And we know that for those who love God all things work together for good, for those who are called according to His purpose."
Romans 8:28 ESV

Romans 8:28 was my Grandma Courtney's favorite verse. She quoted it countless times in her life and that might be the primary reason she was able to endure so many hardships. She was a young bride at 16 years old, had a baby at 17 years old who passed away as an infant, and had another child whose father died in a car accident when the baby was only 9 months old. She was suddenly a very young, single mother and had to go to work while still grieving. She later married again and had 5 more children. These details were just the beginning.

She has long since passed away and I'm sure has been reunited with all who have gone before her. She greatly impacted my life because of her strength and tenacity and her "I-will-beat-it-against-all-odds" attitude. She kept changing her filter – the way she viewed or thought about events and people around her – to keep herself filtering everything freshly. I can't help but believe that her life was better because of her ever-evolving positive perspective.

Like the air filter or oil filter in our car, periodically filters must be cleaned or changed altogether to maintain a good flow of air or oil. Otherwise, our car could overheat, resulting in an unnecessary breakdown and expensive repairs. Having fresh filters keeps our vehicles running longer and more efficiently.

Relationships in life can be tough. Some of the toughest ones to navigate are family relationships - parents, spouses, siblings, and children. Our close friendships are not always easy either.

I have often found that the only way to get past an issue with someone is to "change my filter." This idea simply means to change the way I think about them. For example, maybe I don't necessarily feel the love from someone or maybe I have even been genuinely hurt. To bridge the gap between us, I will eventually give them the benefit of the doubt in order to move on and try to think of them from a place of love rather than a place of disapproval. Essentially, I am "changing my filter." It is a decision that I must consciously make.

Love is not a feeling. Love is a decision. This thinking is a major mind shift that requires some healthy self-talk and some pushing down of pride - not an easy task. And I have yet to master it because I am human and sometimes I just want to be "right!"

1 Corinthians 13:4 (NIV) begins, "Love is patient. . ." and that is where I already have a challenge. I am not a very patient person by nature, but I have learned the hard way that a degree of patience is needed in order to sustain permanent relationships. God knew He would need to spell out the exact requirements for healthy relationships, otherwise people like me would look for a loop-hole!

The passage continues in verse 5, saying that love is, "not self-seeking" and "keeps no record of wrongs" (NIV). These clauses mean "change your filter." You can't be a "history teacher" - constantly reviewing how someone wronged you over the years.

Sometimes we want to be shown love in the precise way that we ideally receive it but ignore the failed attempts of the one trying to genuinely be a friend or make amends. We need to get to a place where we can accept people where they are. I'm not saying adopt their lifestyle or agree with everything they say and do, but treat them with respect and genuinely show them love and receive the love they offer.

This idea is a tall order, I know, but it is possible. I have seen people who interact with each other over the years fall into the same old trap of resentment about something that happened a long time ago. It is almost as if they are waiting on something from the other person, like an acknowledgement or apology, for that relationship to be mended. The resolution they continue to wait for may never come. There must be forgiveness because life goes on.

Let's not waste another minute trying to figure out how to change other people or how to persuade their thinking to be more like ours. Continuously choosing charity and compassion helps you to cherish priceless connections. Commit to love them right where they are and, if necessary, change your filter.

If you have a difficult person who comes to mind, stop and pray for them right now. If you are praying for someone or a situation it is much more difficult to be critical of them. Try it!

Notes:

_____

_____

_____

_____

_____

3 - If God is Sovereign, Why Pray?

"Be joyful in hope, patient in affliction,
faithful in prayer."
Romans 12:12 NIV

If God already knows how everything is going to turn out, why are we troubling ourselves with all this effort to pray? And if we are not informing God of anything new, then what is the point?

"You know everything I'm going to say
before I start the first sentence.
I look behind me and You're there,
then up ahead and You're there too."
Psalm 139:4-5 MSG

God has complete knowledge of my life. Nothing I could say will surprise Him. He knows my heart better than I know it. He knows my thoughts, wishes, and prayers before I pray them. Matthew 6:8 reads, ". . . Your Father knows what you need before you ask Him" (NIV).

Sometimes I pray for something I think I need not fully *knowing* what I really need. Scripture encourages us in Matthew 6:10 to pray for His will to be done. Our prayers should be with that intention - that God's will is what trumps everything else we desire. We may have to adjust our thinking to pray according to the plan He has already laid out for us and not necessarily to pray that He just bless the plans we've made for ourselves that may fall outside of His best plans for us.

There is a saying that was in the church years ago. The story would start out with the telling of someone being in dire straits or in some impossible situation and the people involved would have completely run out of options. Now they were "down to praying" as a last resort. I know this statement is often said sarcastically, but prayer should be our go-to response as a

8

constant conversation with God. It shouldn't be a last-resort, but should serve as a simple reminder that, in the end, everything depends on God and not on us. We win when we wage warfare with the Word – praying our world to align with His will. Perhaps it is in the day-to-day praying that we express our total dependence on God and then He is, in turn, honored by our faith.

Why is persistent prayer so necessary? Because there is a devil who would like to kill you and stop God's plan for your life. If he can distract you with illness, suffering, financial woes, or rebellious kids he will. We must pray against that agenda, consistently and confidently proclaiming the promises in His word over our lives.

> *". . . The prayer of a righteous person is*
> *powerful and effective."*
> *James 5:16b NIV*

So, let's not stop praying. Our prayers don't have to contain flowery words or be long and dramatic. They just need to be genuine. Your prayers matter. God is listening, and He cares about each of us!

What is something you have been too afraid to pray about? Write that prayer out below, jot down the date, and pray over it this week.

Notes:

_____

_____

_____

_____

_____

4- Why Didn't God Make Us Robots?

*"You made all the delicate, inner parts of my body and knit
me together in my mother's womb.
Thank you for making me so wonderfully complex!
Your workmanship is marvelous—
how well I know it. You watched me
as I was being formed in utter seclusion,
as I was woven together in the dark of the womb.
You saw me before I was born.
Every day of my life was recorded in your book."*
Psalm 139:13-16a NLT

*T*hink about it! Wouldn't it be so much easier if God had just made us robots? We would not have feelings, tears, emotions, pride, thoughts, or a will - all things that often get in the way of life. If God had only made us robots, it would be so much simpler, right?

I am not the first to ask this question, but I have pondered this idea several times over the last few years. If God had only made us robotic, then there would be no struggle between good and evil. Problem solved. Hello Heaven!

But God in His omniscience saw ahead in time and knew that we would fail and fall and need Him. He wanted us to be able to choose Him. He wanted us to have the choice to love because He knew that love without choice isn't love at all. He gave us a free will so that we could choose to be in relationship with Him. God giving us a choice had more to do with His glory and satisfaction than it did with our liberty. After all, we were created in His image ultimately for His glory.

Doesn't the value of any good deed go up in our minds if we believe that it is done out of genuine love rather than out of an obligation or command? Of course it does! That must be how God feels about us when we choose Him.

Robotics or artificial intelligence is a popular movie theme. In many of those kinds of movies, the robot starts out with little or no self-awareness, but tends to evolve over time. Writers and producers create personalities for them and they can be "good" or "evil."

In the real world, we are not quite that sophisticated, even though we keep relentlessly striving to create that perfect robot that could substitute as a person. In 2005, someone in Japan designed a real, life-sized robot that from a distance looks very human. "She" can spit out information, but "she" will never have a soul or mind or know God like we can. We've come a long way since then. Many assembly line jobs have replaced people with robotics. Future jobs may be performed by computers, but they will always lack the emotional component of compassion and the gift of creativity.

A robot can be programmed to obey, but it cannot be programmed to love or to respond intuitively. God chose to create people rather than robots to receive that genuine love back from us. Never undervalue your uniqueness. He created us uniquely and wants to be in a unique relationship with us. You are incredibly valuable and there's not one thing you could ever do to make Him not love you or see your value.

We know God has emotions because the Bible uses words to describe God's intense feelings about us like "desires" and "loves." He is actually *pursuing* us, so we must be worth having! God thinks about us. He has plans for us. He loves us. Robots could never replace the uniqueness, complexity, potential, and value of a human being.

Thank God for all the things that are unique about you! Write out some of the characteristics that make you unique and pray that God would use each one in a positive way.

Notes:

_____

_____

_____

_____

_____

5- Draw A Circle

"Make this your common practice: Confess your sins to each other and pray for each other so that you can live together whole and healed. The prayer of a person living right with God is something powerful to be reckoned with."
James 5:16 MSG

Several years ago, I led a ladies' small group where we studied Mark Batterson's *The Circle Maker*. This study encourages you to write down your prayer requests and actually circle them with a big red circle in order to cement them in your mind and organize your prayer life. We prayed for women on a personal level and prayed for very specific needs like physical healing, mending broken relationships, forgiveness, freedom from addiction, and so on. We also prayed for more general concepts including that the people in the entire area where we live would be bombarded with the power and love of Jesus.

Years later, when I rediscovered this specific list I had created, I realized that God had already answered almost every single prayer on the list! It was incredible to see the prayers on paper after all that time had passed. What an encouragement to me and to others to see the documentation of actual prayers being answered. As soon as I read over the list, I started sending screenshots from my phone to whomever the prayer involved, and they were encouraged as well. Since that happened, I no longer underestimate the power of prayer nor the power of the written Word. God was listening, and He is an on-time God.

As many of us learned in school, the main benefit from writing anything down is that the engagement of your mind and your hand is reinforcing everything you are writing. Writing things down improves your ability to recall what you've written and helps you to be more focused. In Habakkuk 2:2 the Lord says "Write the vision and make it plain . . ." (KJV). We can use this same practice for our own prayer requests. Write them down. You will find that you will remember prayer requests so much easier. Making a list will also help you to see all of the things you have prayed for over time and enable you to go back and see how God has moved on your behalf.

Keep on praying and be intentional with your prayers. The power in prayer lies in staying plugged in to the Source. God is listening! He knows us, and He has already searched our hearts. If you don't regularly write your prayers down, I strongly encourage you to start. Just watch and see what God will do! Pray for the seemingly impossible to happen for God can make all things possible.

"Don't worry about anything;
instead, pray about everything.
Tell God what you need,
and thank Him for all He has done."
Philippians 4:6 NLT

This Season of Hope

What are some "impossible" things that God has already miraculously done for you? Write them here and thank Him for that. What else are you praying about this week that seems humanly impossible? Write it in red and draw a circle around it!

Notes:

_____

_____

_____

_____

_____

6 - Reconcile My Life

"For being as he is a man of two minds
(hesitating, dubious, irresolute),
he is unstable and unreliable and uncertain
about everything he thinks, feels, decides."
James 1:8 AMPC

*D*o you know someone who seems to be living a double life? Do they appear to be good and righteous on social media, or on a stage, but in real life they are harsh, judgmental, prideful, and downright mean? Is it you?

Sometimes we need a reality check, a heart check, a checkup with God. We need to make sure that we are living consistently the right way. Are we practicing what we preach? Do we need to make some adjustments so that the way we live in private is the same as what we try to portray in public?

When my daughter was in middle school she was really struggling with who she was as a person. At church and at home certain things were expected of her - honesty, respect, a few chores, and maintenance of her 12 x 12 space. For the most part, she was a very compliant child. After getting into trouble a few times with one of her teachers at school, I asked, "What is going on? Why are you doing things at school that you would not do at home?" She replied, "I'm a different person at school." I said, "Well, you need to be the same person - the obedient and respectful person." Basically, she needed to reconcile her life before it was totally wrecked.

At certain times in my own life, I have felt that same way. I've felt times of inconsistency in my life – when there was a difference between what I knew to do and what I was actually doing. In those times, I knew that if I did not behave in the way that God intended, He would allow me to wreck my own life.

Living a double life is a waste of time. It takes twice as long and twice the effort to try to be anything different than who God created you to be. Besides, sitting on the fence gets really uncomfortable. Make the decision to follow Christ every day no matter where you are.

"Teach me your way, Lord, that I may rely on Your faithfulness; give me an undivided heart, that I may fear Your name. I will praise You, Lord my God, with all my heart; I will glorify Your name forever."
Psalm 86:11-12 NIV

"God has given us the task of telling everyone what He is doing. We're Christ's representatives. God uses us to persuade men and women to drop their differences and enter into God's work of making things right between them. We're speaking for Christ Himself now: Become friends with God, He's already a friend with you."
2 Corinthians 5:20 MSG

I pray that we all may have an undivided heart that is pliable and one that God can use. This is the way. Stay in touch with God like you would a close friend. And, since we are Christ's representatives, we must try to be more like Him and do what Colossians 3:17 says, ". . . giving thanks through Him to God the Father."

"Therefore, since we are surrounded by such a great cloud of witnesses, let us throw off everything that hinders and the sin that so easily entangles. And let us run with perseverance the race marked out for us."
Hebrews 12:1 NIV

Proverbs 18:24 reads, "Friends come and friends go, but a true friend sticks by you like family" (MSG). Become friends with God. He is the truest friend and is there even when you feel there is no one else to turn to.

Do you need a life makeover? Are there some things you need to reconcile in your life? Ask God to show you those places, write them down and pray about them.

Notes:

_____

_____

_____

_____

_____

7- The 80/20 Rule

"But those who hope in the Lord will renew their strength.
They will soar on wings like eagles; they will run and not
grow weary, they will walk and not be faint."
Isaiah 40:31 NIV

You may have heard of the Pareto principle. Wikipedia states that it is also known as the 80/20 rule or the law of the vital few (2018). This principle states that, for many events, roughly 80% of the effects come from 20% of the causes. According to Wikipedia, a business-management consultant suggested the principle and named it after Italian economist Vilfredo Pareto, who observed in 1906 the effects of the 80/20 rule in regard to land ownership in Italy.

It is a common rule of thumb that in business 80% of your sales come from 20% of your customers. It is also found that in most churches about 20% of the congregation does the work while 80% attends and observes.

In life, you may also experience the 80/20 rule when you set a certain life goal. You may find that when you announce something that you are pursuing or have accomplished you get mixed responses for various reasons. Most people will offer their kind congratulations but may not really believe you will ever make it. Yet, there is the faithful, positive 20% who will be with you, cheering you on all the way to the end!

The lessons to learn:
• *Be encouraging!* Don't be in the 80% of people who always state the reasons why something cannot be done.

• *Be encouraged!* If you have set a goal, go for it! Forget the naysayer. They will always be there. Opportunities will not.

Paula Lambert

- *Carpe diem*! Seize the day! Go for it! You're going to walk and not faint. Be the 20%.

> *"So speak encouraging words to one another.*
> *Build up hope so you'll all be together in this,*
> *no one left out, no one left behind.*
> *I know you're already doing this;*
> *just keep on doing it."*
> *1 Thessalonians 5:11 MSG*

Write down the names of your biggest supporters, trusted friends, and close family members - basically your 20%. Thank God for the encouragement and support they bring to your life. Let them know this week what they mean to you. Also take a moment to write down a goal that you are currently pursuing. Thank God for helping you work toward making that goal a reality.

Notes:

_____

_____

_____

_____

_____

8 - Less Than or Equal To?

"Make a careful exploration of who you are and the work
you have been given, and then sink yourself into that.
Don't be impressed with yourself.
Don't compare yourself with others."
Galatians 6:4 MSG

*H*ave you ever been in a situation where you thought you were
not as good as the people around you? Or perhaps you have
been secretly jealous because someone else was getting all the
attention? I guess that happens to everyone on some level. We are
human. Maybe sometimes we even think someone else can do a
thing better than we can. The Word says in Hebrews 13:21,
however, that we are equipped with every good thing to carry out
His will. It also states that He will strengthen us to accomplish
what He calls us to do!

Insecurity is just a trick of the devil that has the potential
to keep us from doing the things God has called us to do. The devil
would like to keep us distracted by making us feel worthless. It's
just as distracting and debilitating, if not more so, than its
opposite extreme, vanity.

There will always be people who are more talented,
thinner, richer, younger, smarter, more beautiful, or more
entertaining than we are. We can't allow ourselves to be
immobilized by falling for the devil's tactics. Being aware of the
strong gifting in others doesn't minimize the importance of our
own strengths. Our value isn't based on a comparison with others,
and knowing this leads us to a better understanding of our actual
self-worth.

This is true humility: walk humbly with God, value others,
have the same mindset as Christ, clothe yourselves with
compassion, kindness, and patience. Insecurity is an emotional
interpretation, not an objective evaluation of our abilities. So, in
theory, two people with the same abilities and skill levels can

experience different types and depths of insecurity. Scripture tells us in Jeremiah 17:9 (MSG), "The heart is hopelessly dark and deceitful, a puzzle that no one can figure out." Our emotions are not reliable, and our perspective is often skewed.

Still there is hope! Insecurity can be overcome when we understand and accept the way Jesus thinks about us. The only way to truly know that is with a steady diet of positive reinforcement from the Word. Then, we can see our true value. We need a revelation that our own worth is purely a matter of how God sees each of us. We can be secure in God's flawless appraisal, which deems us His most priceless possessions. He loves you! He has a specific purpose in mind for you.

"For I know the plans I have for you," declares the Lord,
"plans to prosper you and not to harm you,
plans to give you hope and a future."
Jeremiah 29:11 NIV

We can't see behind the scenes of what God is planning, but we can know that what He has designed for us is good. We have to believe and trust that God is for us. He is really working on our behalf all the time and we are, for the most part, unaware of even a fraction of what He is doing for us.

My prayer today is that those who have been wounded in such a way that may have left them feeling less-than will see themselves the way God sees them. I pray we allow God the space and time to mend those places. If we can possibly believe that God loves us and will not leave us in our weakness, then we might believe that He can also use us to affect others in a very positive way. Don't be intimidated by the strengths you see in others. Break the habit of negative self-talk. Let God be your support system. He is for you!

Did you know that comparison is the thief of joy? Steven Furtick, author and pastor of Elevation church says, "One reason we struggle with insecurity is because we are comparing our behind the scenes with everyone else's highlight reel" (StevenFurtick, 2011). You might even call it "insta-envy" - being

Paula Lambert

Instagram envious. But any social media platform could instigate
this instant, envious response. Don't let it. Comparison is the thief
of joy. Besides, everything you see online is not always as
presented. You are only seeing what the other person is allowing
you to see. Don't get caught up in the comparison game.

*"There has never been the slightest doubt in my mind
that the God who started this great work in you
would keep at it and bring it to a flourishing finish on the
very day Christ Jesus appears."*
Philippians 1:6 MSG

I challenge you to find a scripture to come against every negative thing you tell yourself and combat that mental poison with the Word. You can use the scriptures in this devotional or search for applicable scriptures online. Pray that God would help you overcome those negative thoughts and feelings as you walk this out. Now, write three positive things that God says about you or that you know about yourself.

Notes:

_____

_____

_____

_____

_____

9- What Will They Say When I'm Gone?

"Praise be to the God and Father of our Lord Jesus Christ!
In His great mercy He has given us new birth into a living
hope through the resurrection of Jesus Christ from the dead,
and into an inheritance that can never perish, spoil or fade.
This inheritance is kept in Heaven for you,"
1 Peter 1:3-4 NIV

I have had the honor of attending quite a number of funerals. One thing that always stands out is when the pastor, or other speaker, speaks as if he does not personally know the deceased. When funeral attendance is necessary for a person I do not know, I always appreciate it when the service is over and I feel like I now know the person who passed. I know their good qualities and their weaknesses. I know what they cared about. I can see that people truly loved them.

I always find it quite disturbing when all they can say is "well, he was really passionate about football" or some other external interest. Okay, but what else? One would like to think after someone has lived a full life that there would be something good to talk about that this person has done, something substantive. But many times, there apparently isn't. I then think *what will they say when I'm gone?* Will they say I was a good person? Will they say I made them laugh? Will there by anything they can say about me that would be impactful, meaningful, and lasting?

I have a friend named Cathy. She is native to Thailand and as a child was kidnapped by her biological father who lost her in a gambling debt. The men who won her raped her repeatedly and forced her into sex trafficking. She later escaped that nightmare and grew up to marry a man that she loved. Unfortunately, her husband eventually physically and emotionally abused her and had *her* arrested for domestic violence. She went through years of agony to make her case of innocence and finally won. However,

27

this arduous journey took its toll on her and her daughter. When her daughter was of legal age, she freely chose to live with her father. This arrangement strained the relationship between Cathy and her daughter. During this time, she also suffered a brain tumor that required surgery and faced other serious health problems, as well. Through it all, Cathy managed to attend and graduate from flight attendant school. She has now worked for a major airline for nearly 30 years.

She recently had exploratory surgery to discover why she was having constant migraines and nose bleeds. She received flowers with a card that read, "With our deepest sympathy" from the airline. Her employer, for whom she has worked for nearly 30 years, apparently thought she had passed away! When she told me what happened, I told her, "Now you know what you will get if you really die." This may sound insensitive to some, but you have to know Cathy and her keen sense of humor to fully understand how we could laugh together at that.

Cathy's life has definitely been an extraordinary one. She has a wonderful career that has allowed her to see the world and she is now remarried. Her new husband is a wonderful man who loves her deeply, protects her, and respects her. She is making progress in her relationship with her daughter. She loves the Lord and she is truly an unforgettable person.

What could they say if she really passed away? There would be *volumes* of good things to say. Thank God that this was just a case of a simple miscommunication, but the whole thing made me stop and think. How can we live our lives in such a way that is meaningful and significant?

The best way is to live our lives for God. I know as responsible parents, we want to leave our children something as an inheritance – money, a house, or some other earthly possessions. All those things are good, but the very best thing that we can leave them is the testimony of our lives. What do we do that will truly last? What do they see in us that will encourage them to be more like Jesus and have a relationship with Him?

The real question we should be asking is not even, "What will people say or think about us at the end of our lives?" While it is food for thought, the real question that should be our primary focus is, "What does God have to say about how I am living every single day?" I know He honors a submitted heart and searches for people who are committed to Him. I want that to be what people remember most about me when I am gone – that I lived a life fully devoted to God and loved well those He put in my path each day.

> *"God is always on the alert, constantly on the lookout*
> *for people who are totally committed to Him."*
> *2 Chronicles 16:9a MSG*

Our Hope is in Jesus. If we live our lives totally committed to Him, then that is our legacy and Heaven is our inheritance. That is what really matters most.

Pray that God would reveal every day new ways to live a life that is totally committed to Him. What can you do today that is different from what you did yesterday? Write those thoughts here.

Notes:

_____

_____

_____

_____

_____

10 - Sharpen Your Ax

"Remember: The duller the ax the harder the work;
Use your head: The more brains, the less muscle."
Ecclesiastes 10:10 MSG

Like King David and Samson in the Bible, I too have made some of the worst decisions when I was tired. Now, I realize rest is essential and can be a weapon in the hand of the Lord. The following story illustrates this point very well.

> Some years ago, a young man approached the foreman of a logging crew and asked for a job. "That depends," replied the foreman. "Let's see you fell this tree." The young man stepped forward and skillfully felled a great tree.
> Impressed, the foreman exclaimed, "Start Monday!"
> Monday, Tuesday, Wednesday, Thursday rolled by, and Thursday afternoon the foreman approached the young man and said, "You can pick up your paycheck on the way out today."
> Startled, he replied, "I thought you paid on Friday."
> "Normally we do," answered the foreman, "but we're letting you go today because you've fallen behind. Our daily felling charts show that you've dropped from first place on Monday to last on Wednesday."
> "But I'm a hard worker," the young man objected. "I arrive first, leave last, and even have worked through my coffee breaks!"
> The foreman, sensing the boy's integrity, thought for a minute and then asked, "Have you been sharpening your ax?"
> The young man replied, *"I've been working too hard to take the time."* (Hughes & Hughes, 1987, p.71)

Our lives can be like that story. We sometimes get so busy that we don't take time to "sharpen our ax." It seems that everyone is busier than ever but equally less happy. Why is that? Could it be that we have forgotten how to stay sharp or, better yet, rest?

There's nothing wrong with hard work. But God doesn't want us to get so busy that we neglect the truly important things in life, like taking time to pray, to read and study scripture, or to listen to "the still, small voice of God." There are statistics that show that people who take breaks at work are more productive at the end of the day. We all need time to relax, to think and meditate, to learn and grow. If we don't take time to sharpen our ax, we will become dull and lose our effectiveness. Let rest and time in God's Word be the whetstone that keeps you sharp.

"Jesus said to them, 'Come away with me.
Let us go alone to a quiet place and rest for a while.'. . ."
Mark 6:31a WE

What are you doing to sharpen your ax? Take time to make it a priority. You will be at your best after you have come away with Jesus, taken some quiet time, and rested. You have something unique to offer the world and He longs to see you walk in all He has for you.

"And don't for a minute let this Book of the Revelation be
out of mind. Ponder and meditate on it day and night,
making sure you practice everything written in it.
Then you'll get where you're going; then you'll succeed.
Haven't I commanded you? Strength! Courage!
Don't be timid; don't get discouraged.
God, your God, is with you every step you take."
Joshua 1:9 MSG

What is one thing you will do to "sharpen your ax" this week? Do you need to simply rest? Write a specific action that you will take this week.

Notes:

_____

_____

_____

_____

_____

11 - Mother's Day

*"So don't be afraid: I'm with you. I'll round up all your
scattered children, pull them in from east and west.
I'll send orders north and south: 'Send them back.
Return My sons from distant lands, My daughters from
faraway places. I want them back, every last one who bears
My name, every man, woman, and child whom I created for
My glory, yes, personally formed and made each one.'"*
Isaiah 43:5-7 MSG

What a journey motherhood is! Often as I reflect on my life as a mother, I am moved by the fact that I have a good relationship with my two daughters. How this came to be, I'm not exactly sure. When I became a mother, I was far from a Proverbs 31 woman. To be honest, I went into parenting with no planning; I was basically ill-prepared to take care of any other human being.

I will never forget the day we were packing up to go home from the hospital after having our first-born daughter. I saw her lying on the bed and heard her softly crying. The thought crossed my mind that I didn't have the faintest idea of how to console her. This was a real problem! I was suddenly completely overwhelmed at the huge responsibility I was now facing.

Since that day, and even now, I have been amazed at how God can use our weak and ignorant places to teach us so much about Him! I firmly believe He often allows us to learn about His love by experiencing first-hand the love of a child. We love, give, and forgive because we are motivated by a desire to stay connected to this person who is an extension of us. We see their value.

This must be how God feels! We are an extension of Him, created in His likeness, and He is motivated to know us. He loves and completely forgives us without hesitation at our request, forgetting all the wrong we have done and the pain we have caused. He sees our value. He is surely an amazing God!

34

Paula Lambert

Not only do we learn a lot about God by parenting, but we can learn a lot about ourselves from our children. I sometimes feel as though I am looking in a mirror and it allows me to see exactly the areas where I am weak or falling short. Our role as mothers will change over time, but as long as we breathe, we can learn to be more like Him.

"A good woman is hard to find,
and worth far more than diamonds. . . .
She senses the worth of her work, . . .
and she always faces tomorrow with a smile. . . .
When she speaks she has something worthwhile to say, . . ."
Proverbs 31:10-29 MSG

"Charm is deceitful, and beauty is vain,
but a woman who fears the Lord is to be praised."
Proverbs 31:30 ESV

Write down the names of your natural, adopted, or spiritual children and pray for them. Write down the names of anyone you mentor. Be secure in knowing not only the value God sees in you, but the gains that are compounded because of what you actively invest in others. I also encourage you to thank God for the mother He gave you. Write her name here. If she is still living, pray blessings over her life this week and thank God for the gift of life.

Notes:

_____

_____

_____

_____

_____

12 - Roller Coaster Days

". . . Make the road straight and smooth,
a highway fit for our God.
Fill in the valleys, level off the hills,
Smooth out the ruts, clear out the rocks.
Then God's bright glory will shine and everyone will see it.
Yes. Just as God has said."
Isaiah 40:3-5 MSG

My mother-in-law just turned 82 years old and has been living with Alzheimer's dementia for the past several years. At first, no one wanted to believe there was something serious lurking. But there it was: the diagnosis we suspected and dreaded.

I used to attempt to right the wrongs of all the details in her stories. Finally, after a few years, I decided I had to pick my battles, otherwise we all would end up exhausted and frustrated to the point of tears. But there were things that I absolutely wanted her to know: the family would be there to help her, she could trust us, and we loved her no matter what.

All her responses seem to ebb and flow as Alzheimer's progresses. Sometimes the differences between the highs and lows of the disease make me feel as though I were on a roller coaster ride. There is no rhyme or reason sometimes as to response and behavior. There seems to be no normal or standard. It just is. Some days we hardly know there's an issue. Other days it is painfully obvious. Through all of these ups and downs I have been thankful for a family that is united in our mission to make my mother-in-law's life the best it can be. I'm also very thankful for the family members who live near her and are our boots on the ground for her.

After some strategic planning for her upcoming birthday, we were able to take my mother-in-law out to eat at a fantastic restaurant by this beautiful lake. We toured parts of town that we hoped she would remember. When she started to feel overwhelmed, we all just held our breath. Our big plans didn't seem to have quite the impact we had hoped. My sister-in-law sent me an encouraging text saying she believed that my mother-in-law felt the love we were desperately trying to express and that's really all that mattered.

At times, I've prayed about my concerns and feel like my prayers are just hitting the ceiling. Sometimes I have ideas or dreams that seem so great conceptually, but they don't always work out quite the way I had anticipated. You may feel similarly in that you feel your words fall on deaf ears or there is no change in a situation after you have talked it through and prayed about it. But God hears you. He hears your heart above all of the chatter and noise, cryptic conversations, and through even the simplest prayer.

You may be experiencing some long-term illness or be a caregiver for someone who is unwell. You may be dealing with drug addiction, a bad marriage or relationship, or facing some other difficulty that seems to never end. You might be in an abusive situation or a job that feels like a prison. You may feel like you are in a constant state of grief and there is no way out. You may be having roller coaster days where one minute your child is so sweet you want to cry and the very next minute, they are misbehaving so badly you just want to pull your hair out.

It may feel like no one cares. You are not alone in your feelings. Deuteronomy 31:6 NIV says, ". . . Do not be afraid or terrified . . . for the Lord goes with you; He will never leave you or forsake you." God sees all those hard places and He will meet you in every single place, give you wisdom to know what to do and sustain you.

The Bible mentions "And, it came to pass . . ." many times. If God says it, you can believe it will happen. Your trouble did not come to stay. It came to pass!

"And I will be to her a wall of fire all around,
declares the Lord,
and I will be the glory in her midst.'"
- Zechariah 2:5 ESV

The Lord is protecting you with "fire all around you." No matter the ups and downs you face, He is the strap of security for your life. What "roller-coaster" situation are you walking through right now? Write out what God says is truth about your circumstances and pray over them today.

Notes:

_____

_____

_____

_____

_____

13 - Hidden Figures

"God, investigate my life; get all the facts firsthand.
I'm an open book to You; even from a distance,
You know what I'm thinking.
You know when I leave and when I get back;
I'm never out of your sight.
Psalm 139:1-3 MSG

*I*f you are a movie buff like me, you have probably seen the blockbuster movie, *Hidden Figures.* In this film, three brilliant African-American women at NASA serve as the brains behind one of the greatest operations in history - the launch of astronaut John Glenn in 1962. Early in the film you can see that a great deal of math is done daily by a team of 20-30 women called "calculators." Unfortunately, their contribution to the space program was played down at that time because of the lack of women's rights and racial inequality.

I can't help but think that there are so many people who daily do a lot of work behind the scenes. Whether it is on their job, in their home, on a project, or even in the ministry - many people who make significant contributions go unnoticed or unappreciated. Like the women in *Hidden Figures,* you may play a pivotal role yet remain in the background instead of in the spotlight.

I know people have complained over the years about working together on group projects. There would usually be an initial meeting the responsibilities for the various parts of the project would be divvied up equally, and the clock would start ticking. A week or two rolls by and before you know it, it's the night before the project is due and guess what? Everybody has an excuse for why they couldn't get their part finished. Now it all comes down to you. You stay up all night getting everything together to hopefully get that "A" or any passing grade. The next day the whole team shows up and while you put in all that hard

41

work burning the midnight oil doing everybody else's work, everybody gets equal credit. There's no "I" in "team", right? Life is not always fair and you may never get the credit you deserve, but God sees it!

We all must work for the greater good and give our best. Understanding that it doesn't really matter who gets the credit as long as the goal is accomplished is the right attitude. However, we are human, and we would like to know that God sees all the good things we are doing. And, guess what? He does!

Even if bosses, parents, or teachers won't see your contribution, God does. He hears your cry in the night. He hears the prayers you can only whisper in private. God knows what grieves you, and He is there. He also sees the good you do. He knows what you think, and He knows your motivation. He sees your heart.

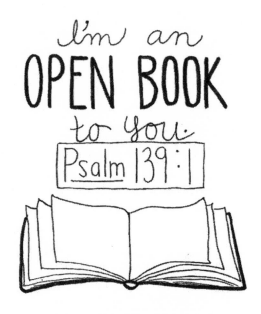

"I've listened to your prayer and
I've observed your tears.
I'm going to heal you."
2 Kings 20:5 MSG

Paula Lambert

When I read 2 Kings 20:5, it is like God is saying "I see you." He created you and He sees you right where you are. He knows you. He cares about you. Even if you think no one notices, His spotlight is on you and you are center-stage. He has a definite plan for your life, and when you seek Him you will find Him.

> *"For we are God's handiwork,*
> *created in Christ Jesus to do good works,*
> *which God prepared in advance for us to do."*
> *Ephesians 2:10 NIV*

Do you feel as though you have been a "hidden figure?" God sees everything in your life. In the book of Romans, it says, "Meanwhile, the moment we get tired in the waiting, God's Spirit is right alongside helping us along. . . . He knows us far better than we know ourselves, . . . That's why we can be so sure that every detail in our lives of love for God is worked into something good" (Romans 8:26, 28, MSG). Write down an example of where you think God has work all things for your good." You will never be hidden from Him. Thank Him for working His plan.

Notes:

_____

_____

_____

_____

_____

14- Only God Makes Things Grow

"I planted the seed, Apollos watered it,
but God has been making it grow.
So neither the one who plants nor the one who waters
is anything, but only God, who makes things grow.
The one who plants and the one who waters
have one purpose, and they will each be rewarded
according to their own labor."
1 Corinthians 3:6-8 NIV

My family and I have lived in the same area in Georgia for the past 25 years. This consistency has allowed me to make quite a lot of friends from several jobs that I held and from several churches in which I have served. I love God's people and I love that we are basically on the same mission as Jesus: to win the lost at any cost and gather people together for the sake of the Kingdom.

When I was a young "pk" (preacher's kid for those who don't know) growing up in Texas my dad pastored several different churches over the years. The churches in our district would often gather for revivals and various meetings. We'd have larger state-wide meetings as well, with representatives from many churches gathering for a general assembly of the entire denomination. I didn't realize at the time how competitive all of that was. The competition seemed to be a healthy one that challenged smaller churches to rise above their circumstances and grow in numbers and in spiritual depth.

Over the years, I've learned to appreciate both the challenge and the unity among all bodies of believers - even interdenominationally. I currently have friends in about 15 different churches in the same area and I absolutely love that fact! I love how each church or ministry takes a different angle on reaching the lost, worshipping, and delivering a message that sticks with you. We don't all worship the same way. We don't all like the same music. We all have different personal convictions. But, ALL love the Lord, represent Christ well, and deeply care about people. I thank God that all of these things can peacefully coexist. This is not only possible, but it is happening and is very effective for the Kingdom!

At different points in my life, I feel like I definitely planted (invited or led to salvation) and watered (encouraged, supported, and prayed for) many people. I absolutely love it when someone comes behind me and invests in the same people that I have invested in and they are able to reap the harvest of all those investments. I wish I could be consistently involved with every person I've ever invested in, but that is not real life. We all have various assignments to carry out – planting seeds and pouring into the lives of others, but we may not always see the end results of the work we have done.

We should not feel deterred if we don't see the harvest of our efforts. Paul talks about this in 1 Corinthians 3:7 when he says, ". . . but only God, who makes things grow" (NIV). How great is that?! We do our part and God does His. We all have a role and we just need to perform accordingly. There is no place for competition, jealousy, or strife in the kingdom of God. It's really not about us. It's about Him!

Don't be discouraged if you see someone you invested in attending another church or involved in another ministry. We are all on the same team. I pray we can all see the value in investing in and loving others of all faiths or those with no spiritual beliefs at all. I love the way God has designed it all to work together! This was His plan from the beginning.

If you are a volunteer for a church or in church leadership, what is one thing you can change about your thinking today to think bigger and be more kingdom-minded? If you are not already volunteering for your church in some capacity, consider taking the next step to invest in someone. Your contribution can make a big difference in someone's life.

Notes:

_____

_____

_____

_____

_____

15- Your Own Skin

"Whatever God has promised
gets stamped with the Yes of Jesus.
In Him, this is what we preach
and pray, the great Amen,
God's Yes and our Yes together, gloriously evident.
God affirms us, making us a sure thing in Christ,
putting His Yes within us.
By His Spirit He has stamped us with His eternal pledge –
a sure beginning of what He is destined to complete."
2 Corinthians 1:21-22 MSG

In my life I have been blessed with many friends. Partly because of the nomadic situation I was in with my dad being a pastor, but mostly because in the last several years I have been very intentional about staying connected with a great number of friends. I have lived in 21 different homes in 20 different cities and I have learned some valuable lessons from every single person I've known. They all individually bring something to the table that I need and truly love.

The number one thing most of my friends have in common is they are very comfortable in their own skin. They know who they are and they embrace every facet of it. I have friends who do not have the benefit of a high school education, yet they are such a joy to be around! You might say they graduated from the school of hard knocks. I have several friends who have doctorates, but they do not wave that accomplishment around like a flag. Instead, they connect to others on more common ground. I have friends in the country, city, and urban areas. They are all very, very human and often deal with the exact same issues. I have friends from a wide range of socioeconomic status and we have learned to help each other. We celebrate birthdays together, baby showers, weddings, graduations, and other accomplishments. We grieve when one is sick or has a personal struggle. We pray for and support each other when someone is needing a shoulder to cry on or just someone to listen. I have friends of different races and ethnicities and I appreciate all of the cultural diversities.

If you find yourself with only one type of friend, I invite and encourage you to broaden your horizons and think bigger. Think differently. Think inclusively. God didn't save us so that we can just sit at home and count our blessings. He saved us for something bigger.

Relationships are the key to making the journey much sweeter than going alone. We are definitely better together, and stronger, and happier! Jim Rohn, motivational speaker, famously said, "You are the average of the five people you spend the most time with" (OfficialJimRohn, 2017). So, with whom do you spend your time?

"It's better to have a partner than go it alone.
Share the work, share the wealth.
And if one falls down, the other helps,"
Ecclesiastes 4:9-10a MSG

"By yourself, you're unprotected.
With a friend you can face the worst.
Can you round up a third?
A three-stranded rope isn't easily snapped."
Ecclesiastes 4:12b MSG

God has already put His stamp of approval on you. He affirmed you. Are you comfortable in your own skin? Insecurity is the just the devil's way of tempting you to sabotage your own life. Don't fall for it! Walk confidently in who God has called you to be and in the life He designed you to live.

If you already have a circle of friends, write their names here and pray for them. If you do not, pray that God will show you someone to trust.

Notes:

_____

_____

_____

_____

_____

16 - This Season of Hope

"And let us not grow weary of doing good,
for in due season we will reap, if we do not give up."
Galatians 6:9 ESV

At various seasons in my life I've gone through some soul-searching times, some financially devastating times, and some deep, emotionally-wounded places. These times were not just for a day or a month. They were seasons that had to be endured. When I was in the middle of any of these type seasons, and I often questioned everything - my motives, my heart, my purpose, endless possibilities and outcomes, God's big plan, and even God Himself.

It is so hard to see God's hand when you're staring at empty kitchen cupboards and the beautiful eyes of children who depend on you. It is hard to see God when your only car is repossessed and you have no idea how that even happened while you and your spouse are going above and beyond to keep it together. It is even more difficult to see God when people who are leaders, mentors, pastors, speakers, teachers, friends, and other good people fail and fail big. But even when you face tough situations, hang on and trust God.

I have often asked, "where is God in all this?" God has a plan, but we have a choice. His plan remains whether we choose to stay on the path or not. We can choose whether or not to trust Him, to ask Him for direction, and whether or not to do what He is asking of us.

He has big plans for our individual lives, but He also has a master plan that WILL play out. God designed this life. He knows how it will all end. In those times of questioning His plan, we have to hang on and trust. I know this can be extremely difficult because we want immediate answers. But if we allow a disconnected feeling to prevail over our thoughts, we risk losing hope altogether. So, don't lose hope. Don't give up. Psalm 30:5 b says, "Weeping may endure for a night, but joy comes in the morning" (AMPC). Thank God for the joy! It will come!

I pray God reveals to you this day exactly what you need to do. Don't get bogged down in the difficult seasons. Don't give up. You have His permission to grieve losses in your life, but He doesn't want you to stay there. There is a time for everything.

> *"To everything there is a season,*
> *A time for every purpose under heaven:*
> *A time to be born, And a time to die;*
> *A time to plant, And a time to pluck what is planted;*
> *A time to kill, And a time to heal;*
> *A time to break down, And a time to build up;*
> *A time to weep, And a time to laugh;*
> *A time to mourn, And a time to dance;"*
> *Ecclesiastes 3:1-4 NKJV*

Don't give up on God no matter what tough or seemingly impossible season you are going through. Keep pressing in close to Him. He is still there. He is still keeping you close. Give it to God and go to sleep tonight resting in that knowledge. Pray for strength for today and bright hope for tomorrow.

Whichever season you're in, you can choose to winter the storms in the shelter of His presence, spring into action at His command, enjoy the sparkling, sunny summer seasons, or fall into His arms of comfort and strength.

> *"God is our refuge and strength,*
> *an ever-present help in trouble.*
> *Therefore we will not fear,*
> *though the earth give way . . ."*
> *Psalm 46:1-2 NIV*

No matter the season or situation, God is our hope! He is with you and for you. There is always hope in Jesus. Write out what you are trusting God for and praying for in this season.

Notes:

_____

_____

_____

_____

_____

17- Road Through the Desert

"This is what God says,
the God who builds a road right through the ocean,
who carves a path through pounding waves,
The God who summons horses and chariots and armies -
they lie down and then can't get up;
they're snuffed out like so many candles:
"Forget about what's happened;
don't keep going over old history.
Be alert, be present. I'm about to do something brand-new.
It's bursting out! Don't you see it? There it is!
I'm making a road through the desert,
rivers in the badlands. . .Because I provided water in the
desert, rivers through the sun-baked earth,
Drinking water for the people I chose,
the people I made especially for myself,
a people custom-made to praise me."
Isaiah 43:16-21 MSG

When a new year rolls around, many people begin thinking about what areas in their life need improving. Ellen Goodman, an American journalist, is quoted (2018) as saying, "We spend January 1 walking through our lives, room by room, drawing up a list of work to be done, cracks to be patched. Maybe this year, to balance the list, we ought to walk through the rooms of our lives . . . not looking for flaws, but for potential."

Have you done that? Do you make your list based on things you lack or areas where you are weak? I know I have. According to one online survey (2017), the top three most common New Year's resolutions in the U.S. for 2018 were to eat healthier, get more exercise, and save more money.

Did your new year start out like that? Those goals are definitely reflective of our culture. I usually start out the year with a fresh perspective, a list of things I want to improve upon, and a series of new things I want to do! I get really excited about new ventures, creating a solid plan, and believing that God is right in the middle of it all. I'm not always successful at making all my endeavors a reality. When something is accomplished, it usually comes after a great deal of thought before taking the first step.

Have you ever made a list of the excuses you give when your life is not like you want? Maybe some of these rationalizations sound familiar: (1) I'm too young. (2) I'm too old. (3) I'm not smart enough. (4) I'm not cool enough. (5) I'm not educated enough. (6) I don't know the right people.

I've said *all* those things to myself, too. Do you feel as though you are looking at your future as a wasteland or a desert? Perhaps you should view it is a blank slate instead!

I want to make the most of every day and I want to encourage you to do the same. What if, for a moment, you opened your mind to the potential that lies within you? What if you considered the power, love, and goodness of the God who lives inside you? What if you asked Him what you should do?

Paula Lambert

"Commit your works to the Lord
(submit and trust them to Him),
and your plans will succeed
(if you respond to His will and guidance)."
Proverbs 16:3 AMP

Write down some new ideas that you have had and pray and thank God for leading you to make those ideas come to reality in this new season. Don't make excuses for why you can't move forward. Instead, pray about the potential and execute the plans as God paves the way before you. Thank God in advance for making a way, a road through the desert, and for giving you new ideas about your future.

Notes:

_____

_____

_____

_____

_____

18 - State of Forgiveness

"Be kind to one another, tenderhearted,
forgiving one another,
as God in Christ forgave you."
Ephesians 4:32 ESV

Several years ago, I was sitting in a conference for the leaders of a church. The all-day session had just started and I must admit my hopes were not very high about whatever was about to happen. After the speaker was introduced, he began speaking about forgiveness. Maybe two minutes into the talk I knew he was talking to me. I immediately had a name in my mind of a person I needed to forgive.

The speaker asked us to turn to our neighbor (who is still one of my very best friends) and ask them to pray for us and say the name of the person we were forgiving!! Uhhh. I wanted to cooperate, but I almost choked on this person's name. The resentment and downright hatred I had for this terrible person was not only justified in my mind, but very, very fresh and real and had rocked on for years.

I did what was asked of me and we got through the short prayer and listened to the rest of the conference which was led by Bruce Hebel, author of *Forgiving Forward*. It was life changing. If you don't have this book and you are dealing with some unforgiveness in your life, I highly recommend it. I thought that the teaching was so important that I ended up teaching a 6-week class on the subject to my ladies' small group at the time.

I had never heard the topic of forgiveness addressed in such a way that not only softened our hearts to what God commands but demonstrated how to take actual steps toward forgiveness and walk it out. Another profound idea addressed was that Jesus died on the cross for all the past, current, and FUTURE sins of the whole world. That means all we have to do is the actual forgiving. Sounds good, right? So, I did it! I forgave this person, left the pain and resentment right there in that room, and made the decision to walk it out. And, I sincerely did! God blessed me and I was able to let it go, truly love that person, and refocus on my own life.

Several more years rock on and this same person for whom I had worked through so much pain and resentment does something even worse AGAIN.... Really? Really Satan? Guess what? I had to go through this process of forgiveness *again* - for the same person - to forgive more hurt and evil, while simultaneously laying down another load of resentment.

I have suffered some emotionally devastating things in my life, even the death of a loved one, but this situation seemed to be the most difficult to work through. It took the longest time to overcome (years, in fact). Sometimes I wish I hadn't cared so much about justice and I could have just focused more on grace or my own condition. The same grace that God offers to us, He offers to the vilest sinner. We have to take our hands off of these difficult situations and let God handle it. We have to accept that He will manage the situation in the right way and choose to move on. Justice is ultimately up to God, not us. I finally did myself a favor and forgave again.

I don't want you to waste precious time like I did, being preoccupied with unforgiven hurt, abuse, or loss. Your life is more valuable than that. Forgiveness isn't about getting justice, it's about giving joy jurisdiction over your heart. God wants us whole and healed, and part of being whole is letting go of whatever keeps you feeling defeated and in emotional pain.

". . . Lord, how many times will my brother sin against me and I forgive him and let it go? Up to seven times? Jesus answered him, "I say to you, not up to seven times, but seventy times seven."
Matthew 18:21-22 AMP

Have you struggled with unforgiveness? Do you feel as though you have truly forgiven those who have hurt you? If you still think of them with anger or bitterness, chances are you haven't fully forgiven them. I've often heard it said, "You don't have to have dinner with them. You just have to forgive them." Exactly.

When you fully forgive, you are fully free! Write down any situation or name of a person you might need to forgive. Release it to God and walk out the forgiveness by making the decision that every time you think of that person you remember that you forgave them. Pray a prayer of blessing over that person right now and remain in a state of forgiveness.

Notes:

_____

_____

_____

_____

_____

19 - Responsibility

"Not that I have already obtained all this,
or have already arrived at my goal,
but I press on to take hold of that
for which Christ Jesus took hold of me."
Philippians 3:12 NIV

I will never forget the spring when I turned 15. All I could think about was driving a car. It hadn't really crossed my mind that I might have to work and pay for one. I guess I thought a car would just drop out of the sky and end up in our driveway. So, as soon as I brought up the subject of driving, my dad started his "responsibility" speech. He told me that if I wanted to drive, I needed to get a job, save my money, pay for the car, keep gas in it, wash it, change the oil, and change the tires on it. He was really stealing my joy with all this responsibility talk.

Aside from some babysitting and hoeing cotton fields in the summer, I had never had an actual job where I paid taxes and got a check. My dad talked to the manager of a small store in town and they both agreed that I could work at fifteen. I was scared to death.

I'm not sure when my dad started to believe that I was really going to work and do what he said, but he must have believed me at some point because a car showed up soon after I turned sixteen. My dad had bought this little green Ford Pinto that I would drive back and forth to school and to my new job. Dad said, "It's yours. Now you have to pay for it." Each month I would make car payments to my dad which included the cost of car insurance. I distinctly remember the insurance being $9.00 a month. I even paid for most of the gas in it. I thought I was Miss Independent.

In my family, we were taught to work for whatever we wanted and then work to maintain it. Basically, we had to be responsible. This concept often seems quite foreign whenever I hear the current news. It's rather mind boggling just how much blame some people put on someone else for their situation.

We have a similar responsibility in our Christian walk as we do in life. Now, I'm not saying you must work for your salvation; salvation is free. I *am* saying you need to give your best effort to do what is right and live a morally upstanding life. In other words, be responsible for yourself.

> *"So don't lose a minute in building*
> *on what you've been given, complementing your basic faith*
> *with good character, spiritual understanding,*
> *alert discipline, passionate patience, reverent wonder,*
> *warm friendliness, and generous love,*
> *each dimension fitting into and developing the others.*
> *With these qualities active and growing in your lives,*
> *no grass will grow under your feet,*
> *no day will pass without its reward as you mature*
> *in your experience of our Master Jesus.*
> *Without these qualities you can't see*
> *what's right before you,*
> *oblivious that your old sinful life*
> *has been wiped off the books."*
> *2 Peter 1:5-8 MSG*

If I blamed the car, my dad, or something else every time I had needed gas in my little Pinto, I would have been relieved of driving. I would not have been considered ready for the responsibility of owning a vehicle. I had to take care of the gas, insurance, and maintenance of the car *myself*.

Thankfully, God has a lot more grace than is humanly possible. However, we all have to take personal responsibility for our own lives and stop blaming other people like our parents, our boss, our school, the government, the church, or even God . . . *especially* God. God wants the best for His children just like great parents do. He will bless us, but the responsibility of doing our part remains on our own shoulders.

Part of being a responsible Christian is being accountable. We all need that one trustworthy person who can simultaneously love us where we are, encourage us, pray for us, and hold us accountable. Do you have that person in your life? If not, ask God to reveal someone who can partner with you in this way. Can you think of ways you can be more accountable and responsible? What areas of your life are the most concerning? Write those concerns down and pray over them.

Notes:

_____

_____

_____

_____

_____

20 - Skeleton in My Closet

"The heart is hopelessly dark and deceitful,
a puzzle that no one can figure out.
But I, God, search the heart and examine the mind.
I get to the heart of the human. I get to the root of things.
I treat them as they really are, not as they pretend to be."
Jeremiah 17:9-10 MSG

Do you have skeletons in your closet? We all have done things in our lives that we now regret or wish we had done differently. And, once we have dealt with it, confessed it to God, and asked for forgiveness, then we are free and forgiven.

Still there are things that we struggle with that may even be secret sin. You might not even know how you got here, but you know you need to get out of it. Internet porn is at an all-time high, and according to research (Internet Pornography, n.d.) 40 million Americans regularly visit porn sites. Other research (Alcoholism, 2018) shows that there aren't enough rehabilitation facilities in the world to handle the 17 million adults who are alcoholics and, according to Origins Recovery (Fuller, 2018), the 47.7 million illicit drug users. If these numbers are shocking to you, just know that it's all around us, but often kept hidden. If you are involved in any of these areas, there is forgiveness and help available. There's a reference list located below for your convenience. Addiction is no longer a taboo topic and freedom is possible for you no matter the current season.

I am blessed to have a friend whom I mentor who has not only survived alcohol and drug addiction, but she is thriving! Her name is Ginny and she has reached this point against all odds and against all statistics. She will tell you that she didn't get here by herself. She finally reached rock bottom in her 40s and had lost practically everything - her job, her health, all her money, her friends, her car, her reputation, and she was about to lose her family too.

After years of different people begging her to consider long-term rehab, she finally consented at the demand of her loving and desperate parents. That day was the start of the best decision ever! Because of her diligence, lots of support from family and a few friends, and the intense level of the Christian-based year-long rehab at Teen Challenge, she was able to slowly get her life back. And she got it back and then some!

Ginny came to the realization that she had a problem that she couldn't fix herself. She talked about external factors, health issues, and family history. She was in and out of Alcoholics Anonymous, out-patient programs, and in-patient rehabs over a span of eight years. But it wasn't until she finally surrendered to God that her life began to change forever. She will tell you she believes there is a hole in the hearts of addicts and other people that only God can fill. It has been one full year since she graduated Jacksonville Women's Center and she spoke at this year's graduation!

We can all take a lesson from this process. First, we must acknowledge when we have a problem. The difficulty we face may not even be one of these issues, but another issue that is just as serious and kept closeted in shame. Then, and only then, can we get the help we need. In most cases, the most effective way to combat these and many more issues is through a spiritual emphasis coupled with accountability on some level. I strongly encourage you to take the steps needed and do what you have to do to overcome any addiction in your life. Freedom from addiction and a life full of possibility is attainable for you!

"Some of you were locked in a dark cell,
cruelly confined behind bars,
punished for defying God's Word,
for turning your back on the High God's counsel –
A hard sentence, and your hearts so heavy,
and not a soul in sight to help.
Then you called out to God in your desperate condition;
He got you out in the nick of time.

He led you out of your dark, dark cell,
broke open the jail and led you out.
So thank God for His marvelous love,
for His miracle mercy to the children He loves;
He shattered the heavy jailhouse doors,
He snapped the prison bars like matchsticks!"
Psalm 107:10-16 MSG

"Think of yourselves as dead to the power of sin.
But now you have new life because of Jesus Christ our Lord.
You are living this new life for God."
Romans 6:11b NLV

You can be dead to the power of sin and raised to life in Jesus! A new start is waiting for you today. That's what God wants for you! Only our Holy God can wholly fill the holes from hurts in our hearts.

Even if you do not feel safe in writing out this sensitive need, please make some mark, draw a symbol, or initial so that there is a tangible reference on this page. Thank God for faithfully directing your very next step to get out of whatever secret sin or addiction you may be involved in. The skeleton in the closet has to go.

If you have a clear conscience on this issue and you honestly don't struggle with addiction, you probably know someone who does. Please write their name and ask God to reveal to you any practical thing you can do to reach out to that person. If that is not possible, please pray for someone else to come into their path to impact them in a positive way.

Notes:

_____

_____

_____

_____

_____

Here is list of resources available:

Teen Challenge - *Teen Challenge offers Christ-centered, faith-based solutions for youth, adults, and families struggling with life-controlling problems, such as addiction. For more information, call 417.581.2181 or visit their website at* https://www.teenchallengeusa.com

Celebrate Recovery - *Celebrate Recovery is a Christ-centered, 12-step recovery program for anyone struggling with hurt, pain, or addiction of any kind. Celebrate Recovery is a safe place to find community and freedom from the issues that are controlling your life. Visit their website for more information:* https://www.celebraterecovery.com

Covenant Eyes - *Our internet accountability service is designed to help you overcome porn by monitoring your internet activity and sending a report to a trusted friend who holds you accountable for your online choices. Please visit us at* https://www.covenanteyes.com

21 - Bang Your Head

"I know all the things you do, and I have opened a door for you that no one can close. You have little strength, yet you obeyed My word and did not deny Me."
Revelation 3:8 NLT

We've had birds become trapped in our garage multiple times. The other day, however, a bird became trapped in the workshop that is attached to our home. The bird was an exhausted wren. She kept trying to fly out a closed window and every time she tried, she would slam into the glass and fall onto the windowsill. She did this over and over until she could barely move.

Birds are really not my thing, but I felt particularly sorry for this one because she could not see the obvious way out. I decided to try and help her. She was so focused on trying to get out of that closed window that she could not see the open, ten-foot-wide garage door *and* the side door that I had opened just for her. After several failed attempts, I finally ended up trapping her between a broom and a paper towel and releasing her outside where she easily flew away.

I couldn't help but think that sometimes we are like that bird - trying to force our way through a window that is closed and we don't see other options for the way out. We often keep going until we are completely exhausted and sometimes mad at other people because we can't be free.

God might be closing that window of opportunity that you see and opening a doorway of purpose that you don't yet see. Revelations 3:8 says, He has "opened a door that no one can close" (NLT). It may appear as if other people are blocking you from opportunities that you think you deserve, but God will open doors for you that will be something you didn't think of or are even unexplainable.

"There is a wide-open door for a great work here . . ."
1 Corinthians 16:9a NLT

God wants all of us to be truly free and He offers a way for that freedom. The way out or the way through may look different than what we expect. God might be making it easier than we realize. He loves us. He is often making a way for us when there really seems to be no way. All we have to do is look for it and walk through it.

He wants to do a great work in you. The door is wide open. Will you walk through it? Sometimes the easy and obvious way out IS the best way to go.

Paula Lambert

In what areas of your life do you feel like the bird that kept banging her head against a closed window? Can you see the open door? Write down some of these areas and what you think God may be showing you about how to walk through them.

Notes:

_____

_____

_____

_____

_____

22 - The Sheep and The Goats

"Then the King will say to those on His right,
'Enter, you who are blessed by my Father!
Take what's coming to you in this kingdom.
It's been ready for you since the world's foundation.
And here's why: I was hungry and you fed me,
I was thirsty and you gave me a drink,
I was homeless and you gave me a room,
I was shivering and you gave me clothes,
I was sick and you stopped to visit,
I was in prison and you came to me.'"
Matthew 25:35-36 MSG

*I*n Matthew 25:31-46, you can read about the parable of the sheep and the goats. This story is really addressing the question of who goes to Heaven and why. Verses 32-33 read, ". . . and He will separate the people one from another as a shepherd separates the sheep from the goats. And He will place the sheep on His right, but the goats on His left" (ESV). If you've never read the whole chapter, then I encourage you to read all of Matthew 25 for a broader understanding. In verses 35 and 36 of Matthew 25, however, Jesus explains how much He values even the smallest acts of kindness we give to others.

I think I had become desensitized to homeless and begging people over the years. So much, in fact that I was really annoyed by them. I was raised with the belief that "if anyone is not willing to work, then he is not to eat, either" (2 Thessalonians 3:10, NASB). And, as it was something with which I agreed, I really felt conflicted when faced with people living this way.

One day, while living in South Georgia right near I75 beside our church, a man came walking up to my husband and me asking for money. We really didn't have any cash and that's exactly what I told him. My husband was a full-time student at Valdosta State University at the time and we made just enough money to take care of our expenses and not a lot more. We weren't really in a position to help anybody else. The man then asked for food. Because we had two beautiful little girls, we didn't think it was a good idea to have him come in for anything. He was turned away and he headed back to the interstate.

Meanwhile, God was working on my conscience. After a few minutes I said to my husband, "We have to take something to that guy." With no further explanation he said, "OK."

I hurried in the house to put together something that looked like a lunch. We quickly made him a peanut butter sandwich, grabbed an apple and a canned drink, and we were out the door. We weren't sure which way he had gone, but we just knew we had to find him. After a brief search, we discovered him on the side of the highway walking south. We stopped and gave him what we had, which wasn't much, but it was enough. He was grateful, and we were relieved.

I have no idea if that guy turned around and pulled a crack pipe out and started smoking or he was so deeply moved by our hesitating generosity that he found Jesus and his best life. I do know we did what we could and what we thought Jesus would have wanted. I can't say by that simple act of obedience that the heavens opened and everything was perfect after that, but I *can* say we were richly blessed that day. Scripture tells us in Acts 20:35 that it is more blessed to give than to receive and in Matthew 25:40 that if we did it for the least of these, then we did it for Him. Part of being blessed means being content and contentment is so desired in this world.

Have you ever passed on opportunities to bless people? We all probably have. And, we can't help everybody. But what if we all helped one person? Showing kindness to others never escapes God's attention. Maybe there is a person God has been leading us to help. If you read the full parable of the sheep and the goats, then you will definitely want to identify with the sheep. Be the sheep!

Pray today that God would show you one person whom you could help in some way. If you already know who it is, write their name here and pray for them today. Every kindness you offer another has potential for a greater impact than you can imagine.

Notes:

_____

_____

_____

_____

_____

23 - Run Out of The Grave

"I have told you these things,
so that in me you may have peace.
In this world you will have trouble.
But take heart! I have overcome the world."
John 16:33 NIV

I have a very good friend who suffered from a debilitating depression for nearly three years. She is a person who was a solid Christian, active in church, a working professional, and married with two grown daughters. One week after her oldest daughter got married, her younger daughter totaled her car and ended up in the hospital for five days and took five months to recover. During that time, her mother passed away. After a 20-year career in banking, she was notified that her company was making cutbacks and her position was gone. While reeling from these life-altering events, her father married a woman he had met on the internet just a few months earlier. Her first grandson was born and her husband was placed on furlough for six months. One week after the furlough ended, she fell and broke her ankle and her home was repossessed. Then, her oldest daughter miscarried and that devastating news seemed to be the final blow.

In just a few short months, her world had come to a screeching halt and she felt very alone in her suffering. For three long years she barely came out of her home despite the begging and pleading of friends and church family. She knew all the scriptures that applied to her situation. She knew the power of prayer. She knew that her family and God loved her, but somehow all of that knowledge seemed to diminish in the sobering reality of life.

Maybe you have felt similarly, and you feel your life is out of control and there's nothing you can do to change it. And, you know, that may be true. Sometimes life happens to us and there's often very little we can do to change the circumstances. My friend couldn't stop the dissolution of her job, the sudden loss of her mother, the insensitivity of her father, the loss of her home, and the loss of her unborn grandchild. As much as she wanted to, she couldn't.

Depression used to be a taboo topic and most people just didn't understand it. They would often dismiss it as a mood or a phase and that the sufferer should just "get over it." Now we know more about the body and although depression could develop from our response to our circumstances, a chemical imbalance could also be the culprit and might be helped with medication. Additionally, we know there is often a spiritual aspect of depression that only God can miraculously heal. Depression is a big deal and according to the World Health Organization (Depression, 2018), it is among the leading causes of disability worldwide with more than 300 million people suffering with this condition. Chances are you know someone who is depressed.

None of the facts in the story about my friend have changed in all these years, but some things *have* changed. She learned to live a life apart from a full-time job. She fully grieved the loss of her mother. She reconciled with her father. She has a home. And now she is enjoying her third grandchild! All of this process took time and slowly God transformed her life that was once stymied by pain and depression. Before she was able to run out of the grave of depression she had to crawl out. She was not healed in a day, but she was daily healing.

Kristian Stanfill, a worship leader at Passion City Church, co-wrote a song that talks about how life's weight can sometimes seem to bury us, making us feel as though we aren't even alive. Whether it is the weight of personal failures, sin, or shame, it is Jesus who calls our name from those places. Mr. Stanfill then writes, "And I ran out of that grave, out of the darkness, into Your glorious day" (Curran, Ingram, Smith, Stanfill, 2017). God doesn't want us to feel bound or buried. He loves us. He wants us to shake off those chains and graveclothes, those things that weigh us down, and live in the peace, joy, and freedom He has for us. He's ever by our side, calling us from where we are to what He has saved for us.

Paula Lambert

Psalm 34:18 (GNT) reads, "The Lord is near to those who are discouraged; He saves those who have lost all hope." There's nothing you can't overcome with His help. There is hope for you. If you are feeling troubled, you are not beyond God's saving hands. He longs to pull you from difficulty until you are completely free from any burden you face.

If you are suffering from depression, you are not alone. Please let someone know. Write out those painful places in the space below and pray over all of them. If you feel comfortable doing so, share with a trusted friend so that they can join you in praying. Take this process day by day so that you also can crawl, walk, and finally run out of that grave of depression. If you know someone with depression, write their name here and please pray for them. Be patient with them. Love them where they are.

Notes:

_____

_____

_____

_____

_____

If you need immediate help or someone to talk to, please go to this website or call this number:
https://suicidepreventionlifeline.org   1.800.273.8255

24- Travel Light

"If anyone forces you to go one mile,
go with them two miles."
Matthew 5:41 NIV

When my girls were about two and four years old, we had just come home from a long Sunday morning at a little church in South Carolina as we had routinely done every week. This particular time, my girls were chucking shoes and getting ready for their Sunday afternoon nap. When I went to their bedroom to see how things were progressing, I discovered a total mess. The older daughter was holding a nearly empty, large container of white baby powder. My younger daughter looked like a white ghost. All you could see were her eyes. They looked completely unsure about what was going to happen next. She, as well as the rest of the room, was completely covered in white powder.

I really wrestled as a young mother whether to scold, spank, or document. I chose the latter. The scene looked like a winter wonderland minus the cold temperature. There was baby powder on every single thing in the room - curtains, carpet, bedding, clothes. My initial reaction was of shock and frustration because I knew who would be cleaning all that mess up. After I took a deep breath and quickly grabbed a camera, I was able to reasonably respond to these two munchkins. They were reprimanded and warned of different consequences for the next time. But the pictures were priceless and as a family we fondly refer to that day often.

You know there is a reason that there are Emergency *Response* Teams and not Emergency *Reaction* Teams. If EMTs, nurses, doctors, and other medical professionals emotionally responded to everything they saw, their jobs would be much more difficult. Their emotional response may even cause the patient to worry and not be helpful at all.

According to Lee Colan, leadership author, "When you simply *react*, your emotional instinct is in control, with little thought of the long-range consequences. When you *respond,* your brain is fully-engaged, and your self-awareness is high. You have the long-term consequences in mind" (2017). When this strategy is regularly practiced, we are able to travel light and know that we responded the best and most reasonable way possible in any given circumstance.

If I had chosen to discipline the girls when they had clearly done something that I did not particularly endorse, we would definitely have had a different outcome. There would have been tears and confusion and probably no pictures to document that historic day. Instead, we remember that moment and are able to laugh at the situation, even though at that time it took me about an hour and several loads of laundry to clean all that up.

Paula Lambert

"Post this at all the intersections, dear friend:
Lead with your ears, follow up with your tongue,
and let anger straggle along in the rear.
God's righteousness doesn't grow from human anger."
James 1:19-20 MSG

Pray a prayer that God would help you to respond rather than react to whatever you are facing today. Make this a practice to travel light and write out one time when you consciously decided to respond versus react.

Notes:

_____

_____

_____

_____

_____

25 - Love Divine

"Let the morning bring me word of Your unfailing love,
for I have put my trust in You.
Show me the way I should go, for to You I entrust my life.
Rescue me from my enemies, Lord, for I hide myself in You.
Teach me to do Your will, for You are my God;
may Your good Spirit lead me on level ground."
Psalm 143:8-10 NIV

All of us have probably been in love at one point or another in our lives. I remember a situation with my daughter when she was about 16-years-old. She had met this guy from church and as far as we knew he was a really good guy. But he was 23. So, with a seven-year difference in age, I didn't care if he was a rocket scientist with a side hustle as a missionary. This relationship was not going to happen. The brain of a 16-year-old has not fully developed and I'm guessing the same could be said of some 23-year-olds.

The relationship, and I use that term loosely, had just begun. That is when we, as her parents, became involved. We had an extremely difficult time convincing our daughter that this relationship was not wise at all. As a mother, I could see how much her choices could potentially alter her valuable future, and as I talked with her, I could sense a holy bridle guiding my conversation. At one point, I distinctly remember her saying, "But, I love him." To her comment I quickly responded, "Love is a decision, not a feeling. And, just like you decided to love him, you are going to decide not to love him." My daughter was somewhat shocked and insulted by this response as she was a firm believer in thinking "love conquers all" at the time.

It wasn't too much longer before we were forced to consider a restraining order. This young man began some unanticipated criminal behavior that included stalking her on her job, tracking her in our neighborhood, and hacking her email account. Thankfully, our pastor at the time was able to talk some sense into him before further action was taken, and our daughter started to see for herself that this relationship was unhealthy and unwise.

Now, if you woke up this morning, you are smart enough to know that this wasn't love. This was obsession and maybe even a little control. No one wants to be in this type of a relationship.

In contrast, the divine love of God is very freeing and His love is the gold standard by which all other love is measured. John 3:16 tells us that God loves us so much He gave His Son to die on a cross for us. His love is sacrificial. He wants the very best for us. His love is giving and considerate. There is no other love that will ever come close to the love of God. His love is perfect every time.

I pray that you will discover, if you haven't already, the astounding, never-ending, divine love of God. He searches for you. He loves you!

If you have had a bad experience with love, don't let that stop you from accepting the love that God has for you. God will never disappoint. God is faithful. God is true. His royal love for you is pure and He has only the best in mind for your future.

> *"Know this: God, your God, is God indeed,*
> *a God you can depend upon.*
> *He keeps His covenant of royal love*
> *with those who love Him and*
> *observe His commandments*
> *for a thousand generations."*
> *Deuteronomy 7:9 MSG*

A thousand generations? That's a very long time. If you have experienced the genuine love of God, write about that here. If you are still not sure if God truly loves you, pray that He would reveal Himself to you in very real ways. During the week, if you believe God is showing you love in tangible ways, come back and write about it here.

Notes:

_____

_____

_____

_____

_____

26 - Double Agent

"A thief is only there to steal and kill and destroy.
I came so they can have real and eternal life,
more and better life than they ever dreamed of."
John 10:10 MSG

Some of my favorite movies have a similar theme - espionage! I love a suspenseful movie where there is a plot twist at the very end that seems to come out of nowhere. These movies are particularly interesting to me because very often there is a double agent reveal that seems to catch me by complete surprise. In real life, I guess I don't understand when people seem to be a "double agent" - one part of them is vying for control, and the other for friendship.

I used to work with a person like that. She would come in every morning at 7:30 am and be all cheery and let me believe we were friends. As the day progressed, however, she would try to drag some dirt out of me with leading questions or twist my words in a way that seemed to undermine the whole department. Then, she would run and report what she discussed with me to the head of the department! After I had been burned a few times by her I learned to just shut my mouth. She almost cost me my job by acting as a double agent.

Those kinds of characters are interesting in film and in books, but not so impressive in real life. Nobody likes them because they seem to have no loyalty to any one person. Their only goal is to divide and conquer in order to benefit themselves. Our spiritual walk can sometimes look like that if we're not careful. We have to make sure our words and actions line up with one another. We must also take care not to sabotage our own life by speaking one way and living another.

Do you know what you believe? Do you know who you are loyal to? Is there someone in your life like my former co-worker? If there is, you can understand exactly what I'm saying.

"Because the LORD revealed their plot to me,
I knew it, for at that time
He showed me what they were doing."
Jeremiah 11:18 NIV

I feel like God showed me what was actually happening and so I stopped feeding that fire. Our conversations at work became very brief and for functional purposes only. I know that's not the ideal environment, but that was the only thing I could do that was within my control. I don't always have the wisdom that God gives, but when I do, I recognize it because I know I didn't come up with that by myself. One thing I regularly pray for is wisdom. The Word says in James 1:5 "If any of you lacks wisdom, you should ask God, who gives generously to all without finding fault, and it will be given to you" (NIV).

So, pray for wisdom in every situation and God will come through for you. My prayer is that you never meet somebody who is acting as a double agent, but if that does happen, then I pray God will give you wisdom to know the right thing to do.

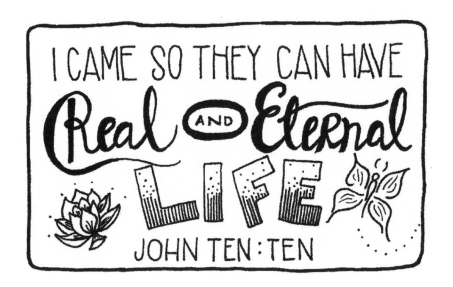

Paula Lambert

Is there a situation in your life where you feel someone is trying to act as your friend, but working against you and you don't know what to do? Write that name here and pray for them and pray for divine wisdom in how to deal with that situation. I pray God will give you the discernment you need and just the right words to respond.

Notes:

_____

_____

_____

_____

_____

27 - Border Patrol

"The revelation of God is whole and pulls our lives together.
The signposts of God are clear and point out the right road.
The life-maps of God are right, showing the way to joy.
The directions of God are plain and easy on the eyes. . . .
Clean the slate, God, so we can start the day fresh!
Keep me from stupid sins,
from thinking I can take over Your work;"
Psalm 19:7-13a MSG

*T*hroughout this devotional we have discussed ways to say yes, to God's plans, to think bigger, and to move through and on to whatever is ahead. In order to do all of those things, we must be able to set personal boundaries. I know that in families, boundary lines can often become ignored or even trampled on. The same is true in business, school, and other relationships. Healthy boundaries define expectations and show respect for others. A boundary is a definite place where your responsibility ends and another person's begins. It stops you from doing for others what they should do for themselves. Through the Word, God has given us many examples of how Jesus himself had boundaries.

Jesus made sure His basic needs were met by eating healthy and getting the rest He needed. He even took naps! I know some people who are really glad to hear that! He had support from His friends and He often withdrew to retreat to His thoughts and have time with God. Jesus always spoke the truth in love and never tolerated evil. He had regular prayer time and was always honest and direct. He wasn't afraid to say "no." He did not allow people to manipulate Him or His words. Yet, He easily relented when it came to the cross.

"If you'll hold on to me for dear life," says God,
"I'll get you out of any trouble.
I'll give you the best of care

Paula Lambert

if you'll only get to know and trust Me.
Call Me and I'll answer, be at your side in bad times;
I'll rescue you, then throw you a party.
I'll give you a long life, give you a long drink of salvation!"
Psalm 91:14-16 MSG

All of Psalm 91 tells us what God will do for us in detail if we trust Him and are faithful to Him. To get a deeper and fuller understanding you may want to go read that whole chapter. These words are very encouraging. What I want to focus on is what we will do for Him. He will do His part. We just need to do ours. Part of that is making good decisions when it comes to personal boundaries of our time, talent, finances, relationships, and just good will. Often in the name of everything good we over-extend ourselves sacrificing our own peace of mind, time with family, and even our health.

Robert Frost wrote a poem called The Mending Wall. In it, he wrote, "Good fences make good neighbors" (Frost, 2014). This well-known proverb means that good neighbors respect the property of one another by keeping their fences in good repair so that one's livestock doesn't trample the property of those who live near their borders. My prayer is that we would allow God to be the "border patrol" in our lives. I pray we permit Him to be the fence around us and allow Him to help us follow the many examples that Jesus gave: spend time with God, eat regularly, rest, spend time with friends, speak the truth in love, don't hesitate to say no, and don't allow manipulation. If we can do all that then we will have established some very healthy boundaries in our lives and hopefully balance, too!

"Lord, You alone are my portion and my cup;
You make my lot secure.
The boundary lines have fallen for me in pleasant places;
surely I have a delightful inheritance."
Psalm 16:5-6 NIV

Can you think of any areas in your life in which you need to establish better boundaries? As God reveals more to us, He will pull our lives together helping us to make the most of what He has given us already. If you can, write those places of concern here. God will be with you every step of the way.

Notes:

_____

_____

_____

_____

_____

28 - End Game

*"All a person's ways seem pure to them,
but motives are weighed by the Lord."*
Proverbs 16:2 NIV

*"Many are the plans in a person's heart,
but it is the LORD'S purpose that prevails."*
Proverbs 19:21 NIV

I attended a homecoming football game recently. The young
ladies nominated for homecoming queen made a statement of
their accomplishments and plans after graduating high school. All
were very similar, but the statement of one girl stood out to me.
She stated her accomplishments that were primarily popularity-
based and told of her future plans. She then said, "fame will
follow." That last part saddened me. Her endgame was obviously
just to be known.

> According to the Urban Dictionary "endgame" is defined:
> The ultimate agenda or desired consequence of a planned
> series of events (often elaborate and unknown to
> outsiders). In the business world it's ideally an ingenious
> business strategy for the purposes of market domination.
> An Endgame scenario does not need to be bad, it may
> ultimately be a miraculously good outcome for all, though
> usually a major component is the acquisition of power by
> the party who planned it, irrespective of the larger
> consequences to others, good or bad. (Endgame, 2015).

So, I ask, what is your endgame? What is your purpose or
motivation in doing the things you do? I know in our current
culture popularity and fame are among the most desirable things
for people of all ages. If you ask the average teenager what they
want to do with their lives, they will often reply, "to be famous."
That's just where we are as a society.

The very emotional stability of some people hangs on the number of "likes" they have on social media. How did we get here? It often feels like the majority of this generation has a *hope* to be famous and maybe even a *plan*. Unfortunately, fame is not an occupation. There are countless positive ways to use fame, but chasing fame and becoming famous itself should not be the end game.

"A devout life does bring wealth,
but it's the rich simplicity of being yourself before God.
Since we entered the world penniless and
will leave it penniless,
if we have bread on the table and shoes on our feet,
that's enough."
1 Timothy 6:8 MSG

I know that 1 Timothy 6:8 doesn't sound very glamorous, but God tells us that what we have is enough. Some people don't necessarily want to be famous, they just want to make a lot of money. At times these people will do just about anything for the almighty dollar. And there is nothing wrong with success. I pray everyone is successful in their life. Unfortunately, I know people on both ends of this spectrum; people who only chase the money and people who find every excuse not to make an honest living by simply working. I can't decide which is more annoying.

"Test yourselves to make sure you are solid in the faith.
Don't drift along taking everything for granted.
Give yourselves regular checkups.
You need firsthand evidence,
not mere hearsay, that Jesus Christ is in you.
Test it out.
If you fail the test, do something about it."
2 Corinthians 13:5 MSG

Just like we would go for a checkup to our physician, we often need a checkup with God. We need to ask God to search our hearts to see if our motivation for daily choices lines up with His Word. What is our purpose for the things we do? Are we self-focused or focused on helping others? Some of us are pretending we are on an island and we need the multitudes to come out and snap our picture. Meanwhile, in the real-world, we are in the middle of almost 8 billion people globally. Everybody can't be famous.

Test yourself. If you fail the test, do something about it. I challenge you to go social-media free for a week. See what happens. I challenge you to be financially conservative for a week. You decide what gets cut out of the budget. You can easily tell what your priorities are simply by reviewing your calendar and your checking account. Some of you may go on seemingly unaffected by this test. Some of you will forget to do it. Some may need backup from a friend. I challenge you to try it! You may learn something about yourself that you did not know before.

Write what your plan is and then come back and write about how the week went. The results should speak for themselves and you should be able to easily identify any areas of concern on your "checkup." Then, pray over those specific areas.

Notes:

_____

_____

_____

_____

_____

29 - Grateful, Thankful, Blessed

"As one psalmist puts it, He throws caution to the winds,
giving to the needy in reckless abandon.
His right-living, right-giving ways never run out,
never wear out. This most generous God who gives seed to
the farmer that becomes bread for your meals
is more than extravagant with you.
He gives you something you can then give away,
which grows into full-formed lives,
robust in God, wealthy in every way,
so that you can be generous in every way,
producing with us great praise to God."
2 Corinthians 9:9-11 MSG

My oldest daughter visited South Africa on a mission trip several years ago and was very moved by the people who were native to the area. She witnessed the women of the village regularly walking miles a day to bring back water for cooking. In fact, NPR (Hallet, 2016) states that 13.5 million women in sub-Saharan Africa take a long walk for water daily. My daughter realized that if they had free and unlimited access to water, there was a good chance that it could greatly enhance their standard of living and maybe even sustain a garden.

She came back home trying to figure exactly what to do about this problem of limited access to water. She decided to start the process of digging a well in the village she had previously visited. This process took about a year to establish a 401(c) Nonprofit called 28Bold, to raise the money to pay for the well, line up the equipment and laborers, and plan the trip back to dig the well. My daughter's tenacity rivals a bulldog. Once she is locked in, consider it done. There will be wells. In fact, the natives of South Africa call her *"Zanamanzi"* which means *"she came with water"* in Swati.

Every time she has returned from a trip to South Africa, she is keenly aware of just how much we take for granted in America. We waste water without a thought. A researcher at PolitiFact (Greenberg, 2016) documented, "U.S. households waste 15 times more food than a person in Africa." We have everything in excess, so much more than we will ever truly need. So just to be born in America means that we are very, very blessed.

Every year, particularly around Thanksgiving, there is a focus on gratefulness. In spite of that, there seems to be a growing emphasis on this feast-fest and shopping frenzy, but somewhere along the way we miss the point of the holiday. I think most people are not aware of the rest of the world and its poverty, hunger, crime, war, and all the dark things that go with those situations.

Knowing that we are very blessed, and others may not be as blessed should motivate us to action. My prayer is that we all are moved by the extravagance of God to do something for others.

"Carrying out this social relief work involves far more than helping meet the bare needs of poor Christians.
It also produces abundant and bountiful thanksgivings to God. This relief offering is a prod to live at your very best, showing your gratitude to God by being openly obedient to the plain meaning of the Message of Christ.
You show your gratitude through your generous offerings to your needy brothers and sisters, and really toward everyone. Meanwhile, moved by the extravagance of God in your lives, they'll respond by praying for you
in passionate intercession for whatever you need.
Thank God for this gift, His gift.
No language can praise it enough!"
2 Corinthians 9:12-15 MSG

With such great need all around the world, it is easy to not want to face that reality and stay self-consumed with thankfulness for our own blessings. But God has purpose for everything, including that with which we have been blessed. Scripture tells us that God gives us something that we can give away (2 Corinthians

9:10, MSG). It is up to us to let those blessings go to work on our behalf for someone else. Organizations like 28Bold go places we may never set foot, but giving our time and from our finances into our churches or other organizations like that one is one way to make an impact on the lives of people we will never meet on this side of Heaven.

This Thanksgiving and the whole year through, I pray we can become more aware of exactly how blessed we are. Write down five things you are thankful for and give thanks for them. How can you help someone else? Where can you volunteer to make a difference? This week look for ways that you can help others out of the overflow that God has given you and write your ideas here.

This Season of Hope

Notes:

_____

_____

_____

_____

_____

If you would like to learn more about making a difference or to donate go to 28Bold.com.

30 - Comfort and Joy

"Oh! May the God of green hope
fill you up with joy,
fill you up with peace,
so that your believing lives,
filled with the life-giving energy of the Holy Spirit,
will brim over with hope!"
Romans 15:13 MSG

When I was growing up in Texas, we were very poor. For that reason, our family's focus was never too much on gifts because there just wasn't much money allotted for that. However, I would get really excited as a child at Christmas because of the anticipation of what the holiday would bring.

Our focus was more about all the experiences that the holiday would bring! We would always see our extended family and celebrate with food, games, music, and even a time of inspirational prayer or personal stories about what God was doing in someone's life. I loved those times!

When it comes to family gatherings these days, much like other mothers I know, I often become anxious because of the planning and coordination of so many generations of people. Decorating, trying desperately to keep everybody happy, meeting specific dietary needs, coordinating sleeping arrangements, enduring everybody talking at once, tolerating really loud people, exercising patience with crying toddlers, and dealing with everyone's individual current mental status can be overwhelming! I really have to psych myself up for it and pray! Yes, pray. All this is going on while we are trying to make a memory and fit in some Jesus! Can you identify with that?

I often think of my grandmother, Pauline, who has long since passed. She somehow would feed everybody who came through the door, lead countless songs while playing a guitar, and seemed to not be too annoyed with the rising volume of voices in her small home with 25-30 strong-willed people. I'm really not sure how she did it all. She was an amazing example of an ideal hostess and I really miss her.

This Christmas season and throughout the year, my prayer for us all is that we would hollow out some time to give to Jesus and be continually mindful of His purpose in coming to earth, the very reason we celebrate anything at all! I also think it's important to make lasting memories and to really enjoy the family that we have. We never know, when we gather, if it will be the last time we see our favorite cousin, our grandparents, or anybody. We need to make the most of every opportunity that presents itself and not allow ourselves to get so worried with all the details that we miss the glorious moments.

> *"When anxiety was great within me,*
> *Your consolation brought me joy."*
> **Psalm 94:19 NIV**

I cherish the memories of every Christmas and family gathering and particularly look forward to seeing every holiday experience through a child's eyes. It's simply precious and priceless no matter what or who we are celebrating.

Paula Lambert

Write down a few goals you have for the next Christmas season or your next family gathering. How can you extend life-giving hope to someone else? Pray that you find the comfort and joy that you desire with Jesus in the center of it all.

Notes:

_____

_____

_____

_____

_____

31 - Losing My Religion

"... What do you think God expects from you?
Just this: Live in His presence in holy reverence,
follow the road He sets out for you,
love Him, serve God, your God,
with everything you have in you,
obey the commandments and regulations of God that I'm
commanding you today — live a good life."
Deuteronomy 10:12-13 MSG

When I was a young girl, growing up in church for me was sometimes bittersweet. I loved the social aspect of church, but I didn't appreciate the rules and regulations. I just wanted to push every single limit. As a third generation Pentecostal, I was expected to meet certain guidelines. I'm not sure at what age I realized that we were different from the general population. I realized I looked different. I stuck out in fourth grade because I was the only person with a dress on and barelegged in December. Girls were not permitted to wear pants or jeans because the church denomination decided it was unacceptable. Because of the practice of this belief, I was ostracized and made fun of by other students. My teacher allowed a full discussion in the 4th grade in front of the whole class where I fielded questions regarding this belief. That experience was very painful as a mere 10-year-old. I was put in a position of defending something that I didn't fully understand, and I was too young to have my own personal convictions.

We call this particular aspect of religion "clothesline preaching" now. Our hemlines had to be so long. Our necklines had to be so high. No jewelry, makeup, pants, or shorts allowed for women. There were just a lot of don'ts that I really didn't care for. This is what religion meant to me as a child.

As I grew up and saw different places and cultures, I realized that the specific religious rules of my childhood were not

Paula Lambert

as important as general modesty. I believe that was what the church was *trying* to do at the time - legislate morality. There were good intentions behind every rule, but something was lost in translation. We often seemed more concerned with those outward things than the condition of the heart. Looking back, the relationship that I had with God often seemed second place to the rules that my religion dictated.

I'm so glad that, in general, today's church culture has definitely moved beyond the emphasis on rules and focuses more now on *relationship* with God. When we get the relationship right, the other areas in our life become more in-line with the Word as well!

There are other ways that I believe we sometimes still act religious today instead of prioritizing our relationship with God. I know some highly educated people who have practically memorized the Bible, but there is no apparent change in their heart or in the life they choose to live. They even fast, pray, and would never miss a service, but they live a mediocre Christian experience because, for whatever reason, they have not *applied* to their own lives the scriptures they can quote so well. They have not allowed God to change their hearts. Why would anyone want to hold themselves back from allowing God to make them a better reflection of Himself?

I don't want to be that person. If we are not ready for change then why are we doing all this? Is it just an exercise to make us all feel better? Is it to assuage our guilt? I think the answer is that we have to lose our *religion* and fully embrace Jesus. If we love Jesus first and have a real relationship with Him, we will want to honor Him every day with our lives. That's how and where the change is made. We will no longer be living out of a place of obligation, but from a place of adoration.

"But prove yourselves doers of the Word,
and not merely hearers who delude themselves.
For if anyone is a hearer of the Word and not a doer,
he is like a man who looks at his natural face in the mirror;

101

for once he has looked at himself and gone away,
he has immediately forgotten what kind of person he was."
James 1:22-25 NASB

As we engage in reading the Word and spending time talking with the One who loves us more than life, we change our focus from rules to relationship. It is then that we remember who God says we are, and we recapture the life He designed us to live.

Do you feel there are rules and rigid guidelines in your life that you must maintain in order to be accepted by God? Do you think you focus more on the do's and don'ts of religion than the relationship you have with the Lord? Spend some time today talking with God about this topic and write one verse that tells how God sees you. He loves you and longs for a relationship with you.

Paula Lambert

Notes:

_____

_____

_____

_____

_____

Index of Topics

Accountability - 59
Addiction - 62
Anxiety/Fear - 97
Boundaries – 83, 86
Choices - 62
Comparison - 23
Contentment - 89
Credit - 44
Depression - 50, 73
Disappointment - 67
Discernment - 83
Effectiveness - 31
Encouragement - 20, 41
Forgiveness - 5, 56
Freedom - 100
God's Love - 80
God's Will - 67
Grace - 1
Gratefulness - 93
Heartbreak - 37
Hidden Sin - 62
Hope – 50
Illness - 37
Insecurity - 23
Justice - 1

Loneliness - 37, 73
Missed Opportunities - 70
Motherhood - 34
Motives - 89
Negative Thoughts - 23
Patience - 5
Peace - 97
Perseverance - 27, 31, 37, 50, 53
Prayer - 8, 14
Purpose - 17, 27, 44, 89
Reactions - 77
Relationships - 20, 23, 37, 41, 44, 47
Responsibility - 59
Rest - 31
Self-Acceptance - 23
Self-Esteem - 23, 47
Significance - 27
Starting Over - 53
Surrender - 56
Trusting God - 50
Uniqueness/Value - 11, 27, 34, 41, 47
Wisdom - 83

References

Alcoholism and Alcohol Abuse. (2018, September 6). Retrieved October 2, 2018 from https://medlineplus.gov/alcoholismandalcoholabuse.html

Colan, L. J. (2017, May 04). Orchestrating Attitude: Getting the Best from Yourself and Others. Retrieved September 11, 2018, from https://www.thelgroup.com/blog/orchestrating-attitude-getting-best-yourself-and-others

Curran, S., Ingram, J., Smith, J., & Stanfill, K. (2017). Glorious day [featuring Kristian Stanfill]. On *Worthy of Your Name* [CD]. Atlanta, GA: Sixstepsrecords

Depression. (2018, March 22). Retrieved September 11, 2018, from http://www.who.int/news-room/fact-sheets/detail/depression

Ellen Goodman. (2018, August 30). Wikiquote. Retrieved October 2, 2018, from https://en.wikiquote.org/wiki/Ellen_Goodman

Endgame. (2015, March 4). Urban Dictionary. Retrieved September 12, 2018, from https://www.urbandictionary.com/define.php?term=Endgame

Fenwick, C. (2017, December 27). Here are the Most Popular New Year's Resolutions for 2018. Retrieved September 20, 2018, from https://patch.com/us/across-america/here-are-most-popular-new-years-resolutions-2018

Frost, R. (1914). Mending Wall by Robert Frost. Retrieved September 11, 2018 from https://www.poetryfoundation.org/poems/44266/mending-wall

Fuller, L. (2018, April 24). Learn the Facts About Drug Use and Addiction in the United States. Retrieved October 20, 2018, from https://www.originsrecovery.com/fast-facts-drug-use-united-states/

Greenberg, J. (2016, October 27). Do US/Europe Folks Waste 15x More Food than Folks in Africa. Retrieved October 21, 2018, from https://www.politifact.com/global-news/statements/2016/oct/27/foodmentum/advocacy-group-useurope-folks-waste-15x-more-food-/

Hallett, V. (2016, July 7). Millions of Women Take a Long Walk with A 40-Pound Water Can. Retrieved September 10, 2018, from https://www.npr.org/sections/goatsandsoda/2016/07/07/484793736/millions-of-women-take-a-long-walk-with-a-40-pound-water-can

Hughes, K. & Hughes, B. (1987). Liberating Ministry from the Success Syndrome. Wheaton, IL: Tyndale House Publishers, Inc.

Internet pornography by the numbers; a significant threat to society. (n.d.). Retrieved September 4, 2018, from https://www.webroot.com/au/en/home/resources/tips/digital-family-life/internet-pornography-by-the-numbers

OfficialJimRohn (2017, December 5). You are the average of the five people you spend the most time with [Twitter Post]. Retrieved from https://twitter.com/OfficialJimRohn/status/938128503467315202

Pareto principle. (2018, July 17). Retrieved July 21, 2018, from https://en.wikipedia.org/wiki/Pareto_principle

StevenFurtick. (2011, May 10). One reason we struggle w/ insecurity: we're comparing our behind the scenes to everyone else's highlight reel [Tweet]. Retrieved from https://twitter.com/stevenfurtick/status/67981913746444288?lang=en

Paula Lambert

About the Author

I grew up in a Christian home as a preacher's kid in Texas. I have lived in 21 homes in 20 different cities, attended 9 schools before high school, attended three colleges, and regularly attended 18 churches in my life. The stories between these pages are from just a few of those countless, colorful experiences. I've always wanted to share personal stories in writing and acknowledge a deeper purpose, and now is the time!

I'm not perfect and won't be on this earth. But just like you, I am a work in progress. I think for too long we have put that perfect expectation on ourselves and allowed it to keep us from doing and being everything we want to do and be. I pray we can let go of that thinking and embrace God with what we have. His mercies are new every morning!

I welcome you to jump into the journey with me and experience for yourself what God can do in your life. My hope is that you find some common ground here coupled with some spiritual truth to encourage you in whatever season you are in. If you haven't already, now is a great time to begin a regular time of devotion with God. You have a very good tool in your hands to do just that.

Look me up in these places:

paulaannlambert on IG
PaulaAnnLambert on Twitter

Thank You

Thank you for purchasing and reading *This Season of Hope.* I appreciate your support and I hope that you found something encouraging between these pages that helped you grow in your walk with the Lord!

If you liked what you read, please take a moment and rate this book online and share your recommendation of this book with others! This book is available on Amazon in print and eBook.

Thank you!

Paula A. Lambert

Made in the USA
Columbia, SC
27 November 2018